The
Secrets
God
Kept

The Secrets God Kept

JOHN VAN DIEST
AND ALTON GANSKY

Tyndale House Publishers, Inc.
WHEATON, ILLINOIS

Visit Tyndale's exciting Web site at www.tyndale.com

TYNDALE is a registered trademark of Tyndale House Publishers, Inc.

Tyndale's quill logo is a trademark of Tyndale House Publishers, Inc.

Designed by Timothy Botts

Unless otherwise indicated, Scripture quotations are taken from the *New American Standard Bible,* © 1960, 1962, 1963, 1968, 1971, 1972, 1973, 1975, 1977, 1995 by The Lockman Foundation. Used by permission.

Scripture quotations marked NLT are taken from the *Holy Bible,* New Living Translation, copyright © 1996. Used by permission of Tyndale House Publishers, Inc., Wheaton, Illinois 60189. All rights reserved.

Scripture quotations marked NIV are taken from the *Holy Bible,* New International Version®. NIV®. Copyright © 1973, 1978, 1984 by International Bible Society. Used by permission of Zondervan Publishing House. All rights reserved.

Library of Congress Cataloging-in-Publication Data

Van Diest, John.
  The secrets God kept / John Van Diest and Alton Gansky.
    p. cm.
  Includes bibliographical references.
  ISBN 1-4143-0048-4 (pbk.)
  1. Bible. N.T.—Theology.   2. Jesus Christ—Parables.   I. Gansky, Alton.   II. Title.
  BS2397.V36 2005
  230′.0415—dc22   2004024175

Printed in the United States of America

10 09 08 07 06 05
7   6   5   4   3   2   1

To Dr. Howard G. Hendricks,
teacher extraordinaire,
whose passion to cause
people to learn reflects the
teaching style of Jesus.

John Van Diest

To Dr. George W. Hare for
teaching me that Bible study
is both noble and necessary,
and for helping me plumb
some of its depths.

Alton Gansky

A Word from the Authors

AS A CHILD, *I Love a Mystery* was at the top of my "must listen to" radio programs. Each week I felt a heightened sense of intrigue and suspense while listening to the continuing tale of three soldiers of fortune who always seemed to stumble into a new adventure.

Today's menu of mysteries available through TV programs, videos, DVDs, and books has captured the eyes and ears of our whole society. We are almost mystery-crazy.

The writers of the Bible knew of our propensity to seek out mysteries and secrets. In fact, the biblical pages are peppered with the unknown, the impossible, the unexpected, and the suspense of mystery and sacred secrets.

The New Testament writers used the "mystery technique" to reveal some of the most important truths of the Bible. The fact that these truths were hidden from the Old Testament period and kept under wraps since before Creation adds to the drama and creates a desire for us to know them and the reasons why they were hidden.

Jesus and Paul both used the mystery form of revelation. Jesus went one step further than Paul and cloaked the mystery-truths of the Kingdom of God in parables, specifically revealing His desire to limit these truths to a select group of people called disciples. Fortunately, we have Jesus' own interpretation of some of these parables.

Robert Fulghum's popular book *All I Really Need to Know I Learned in Kindergarten* focuses on some of the basic but important truths for life. Recently I heard a sermon titled "All I Really Need to Know I Learned in Sunday School" in which the pastor listed four of those needs: (1) to love God, (2) to love the Bible, (3) to love the church, and (4) to love Jesus. Likewise this book could be titled *All I Really Need to Know about God and His Plan I Learned from the Mystery-Truths of the New Testament.*

My level of curiosity about the mystery-truths of the New Testament finally motivated me to take special note of those passages that are introduced by the word *mystery.* Upon initial examination it became apparent that those biblical passages contained the unique notion that these truths were special and particularly hidden from the Old Testament writers and prophets. That piqued my curiosity! They seemed to be designated as key truths, without which much of the plan of God in dealing with men would be vague or in some cases absent altogether.

Upon sharing my findings with Alton Gansky, a gifted writer and biblicist, we devised a partnership where he took my mystery material, added his own study, and unfolded the significance of these "secrets" in book form. Because of our approach, this book reflects his voice, so that when you read the word *I*, it is Alton speaking.

Our collaboration has yielded *The Secrets God Kept.* Alton's writings have taken some rather complex truths and blended them into a clear picture of God's unique plan for man—now we can know some of God's thoughts and actions in the unfolding drama of redemption.

Others who have contributed significantly to this book include Jan Long Harris, who from the get-go showed enthusiasm for this project and offered valuable suggestions, and Kim Miller, gifted writer and editor, whose skills are evident on the pages of this book.

WARNING—The gold, silver, and platinum truths in this book need mining skills beyond the casual, haphazard approach to Bible study. As someone said to me recently, "This is big stuff." But the reward is worth it.

John Van Diest

ONE of the most thrilling moments in my life came when I accepted an invitation to tour the USS *Salt Lake City* (SSN 716) in San Diego, California. I had become interested in submarines while researching my novel *A Ship Possessed*. To be able to walk the companionways of the 360-foot-long, Los Angeles Class, fast attack submarine was a dream come true. I toured the torpedo rooms, looked through one of the high-tech periscopes, and peeked into the officer's wardroom.

In the control room, our guide allowed me to sit at one of the helm stations. It was humbling to realize that I had no idea what I was looking at. I knew that one station controlled the depth of the submarine while the other controlled direction, but beyond that, I was awash in ignorance. My lack of knowledge nearly got me into trouble.

When civilians with no security clearance tour a vessel like the *Salt Lake City*, they hear that some places are off-limits. We were not to touch anything without permission, and wandering off was forbidden. When I sat in the chair, I noticed the gauges before me. I also noticed that a few had black plastic covers over them, concealing the face of the indicators. My first impulse was to reach forward and pull a plastic cover off to see what lay behind it. Thankfully, my reason returned. I learned the hidden gauges were for speed and depth and the covers were in place for a reason—the information was top secret and not meant for eyes like mine. The navy has its secrets and wasn't about to reveal them to me.

Through the history of humankind, God has revealed Himself. Those who come to Him in faith can learn great and wondrous things, but no human knows it all. We are undertaking a journey together in this book, a trip that requires a little work, some thought, and even some prayer. Like the navy, God has had His secrets, and with the coming of Christ and the church age, some of those secrets are now available to us. The Bible uses the word *mystery*, a term with a very specific meaning, to describe those secrets.

Ahead lay some thoughtful challenges. In some cases, we are going to answer questions you may not know you had. The journey before us is interesting because it deals with the very nature of God and His plan for our lives, our world, and His Kingdom.

God has invited us to look at matters that Old Testament heroes saw only dimly. Jesus has brought those things into the bright sunlight. Join us as we peek at some of God's secrets–secrets He wants us to see.

Alton Gansky

Where's the Mystery?

IT HAS ALL the makings of a good riddle: What cost $1.5 billion dollars, weighs 24,500 pounds, and is the size of a school bus? Did you guess the Hubble Space Telescope? In April 1990, this famous device took its place in orbit around Earth. Every ninety-seven minutes it completes one orbit and to do so it must travel at 17,500 miles per hour at an altitude of 353 miles. It is impressive in every way. Each day it collects so much data through its telescopic eye that it would take 10,000 computer diskettes to hold it all.[1] Scientists began designing this system in the 1970s, all so we could look beyond our solar system and see what lies beyond our sight.

Despite some early problems, the Hubble Telescope has worked admirably. Each time it takes a photo of some distant galaxy or area of space, it is looking *back* in time. The light that travels through space and into the telescope reveals what once was, not what is. Still we look, because looking is part of human nature. Woven into the fabric of our thoughts is an unyielding desire to know.

It is nothing new.

Two millennia ago a small group of followers listened to a series of sermons that often left them with questions. The Teacher was Jesus and His message was simple yet sometimes difficult to absorb. The disciples were faithful followers, soaking up as much as they could but often feeling as if they had missed something.

Jesus confounded the teaching of the religious leaders and pointed His listeners' attention back to the God of the Old Testament. To understand what Jesus was teaching, His disciples had to look from the present to the past. There in the long ago were the likes of Abraham, Moses, Daniel, Elijah, David, Solomon, Noah, and others who would make up a biblical hall of fame.

Since childhood Jesus' followers had heard the accounts of Moses raising his staff over the Red Sea so that God could make a path of escape for the children of Israel; of God using His own hand to write the Ten Commandments and calling Moses up the mountain to receive them; of God responding to Elijah's call with a bolt of consuming fire from heaven; of David calling upon the name of the Lord before engaging yet another enemy in battle; of God appearing to Solomon after he and the Israelites spent fourteen days celebrating the completion of God's Temple—all great events to meditate upon. But that's all they seemed to be. Moses lived 1,400 years before Peter and the other disciples. That's a very long time. God had worked powerfully through these giants of the Scriptures, but what could He do through them? Still, like all Jews of their day, they would have looked through those foggy years of history with admiration for men so dedicated to God; men whom God had chosen to do, see, and know great things.

That's why something Jesus said must have shaken them to the marrow.

Jesus had had a full morning of teaching, healing, and the always-burdensome task of enduring criticism. He stood on the shore of the Sea of Galilee where crowds gathered. As the crowds pressed in, Jesus entered a fishing boat with His disciples. From the boat, with the water to separate Him from the pressing congregation, with a disciple on each of the four oars and one on the tiller, Jesus began to teach in parables. However, it was the private statement made later that would astonish them. "For truly I say to you, that many prophets and righteous men desired to see what you see, and did not see it; and to hear what you hear, and did not hear it" (Matthew 13:17).

It is easy to imagine the hush that followed that sentence. Our eyes travel over the words quickly, but the disciples would have been stunned. Jesus was revealing truth to them that had been kept from the great heroes of the faith. It's quite likely that these followers already wondered why Jesus had chosen such an odd mix of characters to be His disciples. They were nothing like the heroes of old. These leaders-to-be were not even drawn from the ranks of religious intellectuals or priests. They were not theologians. They were a composite of roughneck fishermen, a tax collector, and even one from the political activist group known as the Zealots—a sect of Jews opposed to Roman occupation who rebelled by refusing to pay taxes. (It is interesting to think of the early days of the disciples and what discussions might have taken place between the former tax collector Matthew and the former Zealot Simon.)

This ragtag group would change the world. *We* know that, but at the time Jesus uttered those words that truth may not have been clear to them. If it wasn't, then the Lord's statement should have helped them along the path of understanding.

But we can't stop there, because there is subtlety between the lines. The blazing reality that the disciples were unique in all of history makes it hard to see that there is an unstated truth: The saints that preceded the disciples didn't have the complete picture. They had the "big picture," but some things hung just beyond sight. They did not see what the disciples would see.

Years later, at the end of Paul's letter to the Romans, the apostle reminded his audience of this: Jesus was the one who revealed God's plan to bring salvation to the Gentiles as well as the Jews "according to the revelation of the mystery which has been kept secret for long ages past, but now is manifested, and by the Scriptures of the prophets, according to the commandment of the eternal God" (Romans 16:25-26). In other words, the Old Testament prophets had foretold of Christ and His message without having a full understanding of their words. Only now, after Christ's coming, was this mystery revealed.

A WORD BY ANY OTHER DEFINITION . . .

Everyone loves a good mystery.

But better than a good mystery is a *God* mystery.

Say the term *mystery* and images of suspense-filled books, movies, and television shows might come to mind. Agatha Christie wrote over seventy whodunits; Sue Grafton and Tony Hillerman have made millions writing popular mysteries. In a murder mystery, the reader sees all the clues but the author leaves them in the dark until the end. No wonder that today when we hear the word *mystery*, we assume it means something hidden from our knowledge, purposely tucked away from our prying eyes.

Oddly, a biblical mystery is the opposite of what we expect. Contemporary English uses *mystery* to mean that something is *concealed*; but the Bible uses the term to mean something that has been *revealed*. It isn't the covering over of a truth, but its divine revelation.

New Testament authors wrote in a type of Greek common to the people of Jesus' day–a powerful, precise, and detailed language. Furthermore, the words that appear in the New Testament text are not there by accident but by inspiration. Consequently, some words demand extra attention. The Greek word translated *mysteries*[2] is just such a word.

Because our English translations render the Greek *musterion* as mystery or secret, with the root word meaning "to shut something up, as in to hide," we can easily miss the distinction the New Testament writers were trying to make: God has chosen to reveal some secrets that had been hidden from the Old Testament saints.

Not only that, but these revealed truths would be incomprehensible to those listeners, like many of the Pharisees, who closed their mind to the gospel message. Although the word *mysteries* appears twenty-seven times in the New Testament, the only time Jesus utters it is when He tells his bewildered disciples that they would "know the *mysteries* of the kingdom of heaven." (Matthew 13:11, Mark 4:11, and Luke 8:10 record the same event.)

We stand two thousand years removed from Jesus'

comment. We, like the Hubble Telescope, are looking back so we can better understand the present and the future. We have much more written history, thousands of archeological artifacts to examine, volumes of ancient literature to study, and enough science books to fill a stadium, but all of them are secondary to the importance of what God has revealed–and He has revealed much. (Keep in mind that in this book we don't offer answers to such questions as "How did Jesus perform his miracles?" or "What will the end times be like?" Instead we focus on those truths that God once purposely hid but has now made known in His Word.)

Yet even today Christians often miss the implication of what Jesus revealed through His teaching and what the apostles made known in their letters. Oh, we may have the New Testament story lines and timelines down pat, but do we understand how Jesus' words can radically impact our lives, can make us live with "wonderful expectation" as we consider our "priceless inheritance" (1 Peter 1:3-4, NLT).

After Peter told the severely persecuted recipients of his first letter to live with hope and joy, he added: "Your reward for trusting him will be the salvation of your souls. This salvation was something the prophets wanted to know more about. They prophesied about this gracious salvation prepared for you. . . . They were told that these things would not happen during their lifetime, but many years later, during yours" (vv. 9-10, 12, NLT).

So what's the value of taking this journey back to the pages of a book written two thousand years ago to reexamine passages that may be familiar to you? Consider the story told by Russell H. Conwell, founder of Temple University, who once traveled with a camel caravan in a valley between the Tigris and Euphrates Rivers. To pass the time, the guide told stories to the American tourists traveling with him. One story was about a wealthy Persian farmer lured away from the prosperity he already had to search the world for diamonds. He died frustrated and impoverished. But the new owner of the farmer's home and lands discovered a shiny stone in a creek that ran through the garden. That stone turned out to be just one of hundreds of diamonds discovered on the property. Conwell was so impressed by this story that he included it in a lecture he called "Acres of Diamonds." It proved so popular that he gave that same speech over six thousand times.[3]

The story's poignant and powerful moral stuck with Conwell and inspired thousands of others who heard the story. We all suspect—even hope—that we could find "diamonds" in our own lives, if only we knew where to look.

The Bible is loaded with treasure. It is filled with truth and wisdom, power and motivation, but is often overlooked because many fail to see the wealth it contains.

The mysteries of the Bible are some of these riches. What lies ahead is insight into what God has done, is doing, and is going to do. There is the adventure. There is the benefit. There is the reason we should explore what "many prophets and righteous men desired to see . . . and did not see" (Mathew 13:17).

God has revealed the secrets; let's get to know them.

FOR REFLECTION

1. What is the distinctiveness of the Bible mysteries we will discuss in this book? How does the meaning of the word *mystery* in this book differ from the way we ordinarily use that term?

2. In which Testament of the Bible are these secrets revealed?

3. In the Old Testament, who were given some details about the mysteries that would be revealed later? How do the apostles describe their role—and the limitations under which these men worked? (See Romans 16:25-26 and 1 Peter 1:9-12.)

4. What value do you think considering the "secrets God kept" might have in your life?

PART ONE

The God of Mystery

CHAPTER 1

Why Does God Keep Secrets?

The truth must dazzle gradually / Or every man be blind.

EMILY DICKINSON

Then the LORD answered Job out of the whirlwind and said, "Who is this that darkens counsel by words without knowledge? Now gird up your loins like a man, and I will ask you, and you instruct Me! Where were you when I laid the foundation of the earth? Tell Me, if you have understanding. . . ." Then Job answered the LORD and said, . . . "I have declared that which I did not understand, things too wonderful for me, which I did not know."

JOB 38:1-4; 42:1, 3

T HE eighteenth-century poet William Cowper was a troubled, sometimes suicidal man who gained some relief in writing beautiful poetry. His most famous poem, now a familiar hymn, begins with the lines:

> *God moves in a mysterious way,*
> *His wonders to perform;*
> *He plants His footsteps in the sea,*
> *And rides upon the storm.*

That first line is so popular, in fact, that people often ask pastors where they can find it in the Bible. Those words are not part of the biblical text but the concept certainly is. God is mysterious to the human mind. It stuns some to learn that God keeps secrets. Over three thousand years ago, Moses wrote, "The secret things belong to the LORD our God, but the things revealed belong to us and to our sons forever, that we may observe all the words of this law" (Deuteronomy 29:29). Yes, God keeps secrets, but He also reveals a great deal to us. King Solomon said, "It is the glory of God to conceal a matter, but the glory of kings is to search out a matter" (Proverbs 25:2).

Realizing that God keeps secrets sometimes troubles us.

Perhaps that is because we often view a secret as being something dishonest. But secrecy is not inherently dishonest. Parents keep secrets from their children, often because the children are too young to understand. There is a reason parents do not share the facts of life with a five-year-old. In most families, parents don't discuss the family finances with young teenagers. As we keep secrets from children who are not ready for the facts, so God keeps His secrets.

A LOOK AT GOD'S WATCH

Our understanding of God is further limited by the reality of living within the confines of time. Just think how tightly our lives are connected to it. In the winter of 2004, NASA successfully landed two robot explorers on Mars, a planet over 100 million miles away. Communication was vital to the success of the mission and the ability of NASA and others to download pictures of the red planet. But Mars time isn't the same as Earth time. Its day is just over half an hour longer than ours is. Special watches geared to Martian time were given to the engineers and scientists to help them keep track of time on Mars—a special watch for a special occasion.

If God had a watch (not that He would need one), it would certainly be different from those we wear. We measure our days in hours, our years in months, and our lives in decades. Naturally, our view of time is different from the Creator's. It would have to be. Our sense of time is limited; God's is not. Our timeline is one dimensional, moving from the present into the future. We created beings are confined to the moment and have no power to move ahead or behind. Time passes whether we wish it to or not.

God has a different perspective. He knows the beginning from the end and is able to spend an eternity in a moment or watch a millennium pass in the blink of an eye. While we are slaves to the passage of time, He is its master. Consequently, God's view of things is very different from ours. Many of the mysteries—those things formerly hidden but now revealed— were unveiled at specific times for reasons known only to God. Humans are time bound, but God is unrestricted.

When Satan tempted Jesus the Scriptures record: "And he led Him up and showed Him all the kingdoms of the world in a moment of time" (Luke 4:5). Apparently even Satan works in a different time than we do.

We are chauvinistic about time. It's natural. It's normal. But it is also limiting. God works in the "right" time. His watch ticks differently than ours. His plan is on schedule. The apostle Paul wrote: "But when the fullness of the time came, God sent forth His Son, born of a woman, born under the Law, in order that He might redeem those who were under the Law, that we might receive the adoption as sons" (Galatians 4:4-5).

We have a sense of right time. We know how long a human pregnancy should last; farmers understand how long it takes corn to grow sweet and ready for harvest; we know how long we should sleep. What we don't have is a full grasp of God's timing. When Jesus was born, He was born in the right place at the right time in the right country that was ruled by the right empire, all of which worked together to make it possible for the gospel to flourish. It was neither accident nor coincidence. It was part of God's well-timed plan.

In his book *The School of Dying Graces,* Richard Felix explores the lessons for living that he learned from his wife's battle against cancer. One of those lessons had to do with gratitude for the beauty and mystery of life, even in the midst of suffering. Just a few months before her death, Richard and his wife, Vivian, were moved by a sermon called "Kingdom Come Vision" by Pastor Jack Hayford. Richard Felix later reflected:

> *In the original Greek, the word [mystery] carries a connotation of a slow unveiling. What was once hidden is now* in the process of *being revealed. . . . Such mystery slowly–often painfully slowly–unfolds. In the canvas of humanity, God has to weave an eternity of souls and needs. If we fail to see with the eyes of faith, the mystery seems either to unravel, stall, or worse, mutate. Because God exists in eternity, Dr. Hayford continued, we are tempted to despise waiting through the long days of our*

suffering. It is not surprising, then, that one of God's most frequent requests is to "wait on me."[1]

Not only do the limits of our minds and our confinement within time restrict our understanding, but God conceals some truths from us for another, more personal, reason. He keeps secrets for those who care to inquire, who long to relate to Him as their Father and Friend.

In that sense, godly secrets are incentives. As an enemy's army was sacking Jerusalem, leaving the prophet Jeremiah confined to a palace courtyard, God assured him of his presence and help: "Ask me and I will tell you remarkable secrets you do not know about things to come" (Jeremiah 33:3, NLT).

When I first began to dabble in writing, I tried my hand at short story fiction. Influenced by years of reading science fiction, it seemed natural to launch out in that genre. My first effort was a miserable little tale with an odd twist. I told of scientists who had made contact with an alien race living twenty light-years away. Since communication was expensive and took two decades to complete, they decided they could send only one question. After months of debate, they settled on, "What do you value most?"

Years passed as they waited for the reply. On the day they expected to hear back, they gathered the finest minds from science, theology, and philosophy to discuss the possible responses and the impact they would have on society. Each group had their own view. Medical doctors were certain that a formula to cure all diseases would be sent; philosophers believed that they would hear words of truth; theologians speculated about the alien view of God; and scientists were sure that an equation balancing all the forces of nature could be the only answer.

The reply was short: "What do you value most? Privacy." The transmission ended.

One of the great joys of life is realizing that God prefers conversation to privacy. Our God is not a hermit. He is the author of communication and He reveals information about Himself and His plans. Had I written that story with us asking

God to name one thing He values most, I would have written His answer as "Fellowship." He longs for the unbroken fellowship He enjoyed with Adam and Eve in the Garden before the Fall, when the first man and woman could walk with Him, feeling no shame, no fear, no separation.

In short, He wants you to know Him intimately, as a friend and His son or daughter. Facts are good; but experience is better. As J. I. Packer said, "A little knowledge *of* God is worth more than a great deal of knowledge *about* Him" (emphasis mine).[2] God has no desire to be the subject of human scrutiny. His goal is for us to know Him in a personal way, not in the abstract.

Unfortunately, we live in a world that seems hung up on facts. John Eldredge sums it up this way:

> *We children of the Internet and the cell phone and the Weather Channel, we think we are the enlightened ones. We aren't fooled by anything–we just want the facts. The bottom line. So proposition has become our means of saying what is true and what is not. . . . God loves you; you matter to him. That is a fact, stated as a proposition. I imagine most of you have heard it any number of times. Why, then, aren't we the happiest people on earth? It hasn't reached our hearts. Facts stay lodged in the mind, for the most part. They don't speak at the level we need to hear.*[3]

Jesus encountered that problem with the Pharisees, Sadducees, and scribes. They knew a great deal about God, but knew very little of Him. That prompted Jesus to say, "You know neither Me nor My Father; if you knew Me, you would know My Father also" (John 8:19). Head knowledge can be of great benefit–but only if we combine it with sincere heart knowledge. Knowing *of* God is not the same as *knowing* God.

The spiritual life is two journeys: one *to* God, the other *in* God. We are familiar with the first. The belief in a Supreme Being is part of every culture and every epoch of history. There is an innate desire to connect with something greater than we are. Enticing but empty belief systems can sidetrack us. We can seek to fill the void with material possessions or be seduced by comfortable and undemanding spiritual pabulum that makes us feel spiritual but leaves us without the crucial element of relationship. A survey of the teachings found in the Bible is summed up in a single, simple sentence: God desires a relationship with you. All of revelation is about the distance sin has put between God and His created ones and God's effort to bring those whom He loves back into a vital bond.

To make all this possible, Jesus became a member of a poor Jewish family in the same way we all enter a family—He was born into it. After laboring in obscurity in a carpenter's shop for most of His life, He spent three busy years in ministry before His provocative teachings and miracles led the religious leaders to demand His death. How smugly His enemies must have walked away from His body on the cross, only to discover three days later that Jesus had slipped the bonds of death. When we believe Jesus' claim that He came to be our Savior and throw ourselves on His mercy, a relationship with God is possible. But that's only the beginning. That is the journey *to* God. There is also a journey *in* God.

We don't make this journey all at once. Unlike computers that can download great amounts of information from the Internet, humans cannot "download" knowledge of God. Knowing God is not an event, but a process. It also is interactive. That is the power of Jesus' parables: They engage the mind. Jesus did not teach by rote. He never said to His followers, "Here, memorize these twenty passages of Scripture." He taught by example, He taught by principle, and He taught by illustration.

One of the most famous train routes in the United States runs through the Tehachapi Mountains in southern California. It winds around smooth, oak tree–decorated hills. In one of the mountains is a tunnel. You can stand above the exit point of the tunnel and watch a train emerge, one car clanking after another. God's revelation is similar to watching that train. Every train car is like a new revelation from God. We can look into the past and see which cars have emerged from the tunnel opening, but our perch above the tunnel prevents us from seeing how long the train is. The heroes of the Old Testament saw and experienced many things, but they also longed to know what was to come–they would have loved to see the end of the revelation train.

Jesus told the disciples that what was a mystery to the saints of old was going to be common knowledge for them. The same is true for us. What has gone on before, God has revealed for our benefit. God has revealed more than enough to keep us busy for this lifetime, but some things He has withheld until the right time–and only He knows what the right time is.

Perhaps what should puzzle us is not that God has secrets, but that He has shared some of those secrets with us. Those things God has shared are ours to hold, use, think upon, share, mull over, chew on, cling to, and teach to others. They are gems of revelation meant to enrich us in this life and the next.

Shrouded as the details of the future may be, God's will–His plan for us through Jesus Christ–has never been clearer. What Moses wished to see; what Elijah longed to know; what other great biblical heroes hungered for, we have. Jesus and the apostle Paul unveil many of God's plans in the Bible.

God has revealed the secrets; let's get to know them. All we have to do is look.

FOR REFLECTION

1. Suggest some reasons God keeps secrets.
2. David spent many years running from King Saul, who was bent on killing him. Many of his psalms testify to his feelings of helplessness and fear during this time. One lesson God taught him is found in Psalm 37:7 and Psalm 40:1. Can you identify it? How might this lesson have helped him (and in turn help us) deal with the realization that there is so much we do not know?
3. What does the Bible tell us about God's timing? (See Romans 5:6 and Galatians 4:4-5.)

4. Do you agree that God's secrets serve as incentives for those who desire to know Him better? If yes, how so?

5. What are the differences between *knowing about* God and *knowing* Him personally?

CHAPTER 2

The Mystery of God's Will

The end of life is not to deny self, nor to be true, nor to keep the Ten Commandments—it is simply to do God's will.

HENRY DRUMMOND

He made known to us the mystery of His will, according to His kind intention which He purposed in Him with a view to an administration suitable to the fullness of the times, that is, the summing up of all things in Christ, things in the heavens and things on the earth.

EPHESIANS 1:9-10

TODAY the great physicist Albert Einstein is remembered for his wild hair and his famous equation "$E = mc^2$." What has largely been forgotten is Einstein's keen interest in social issues. Early in his career, he was enthusiastic about the prospects of science making mankind better and bringing us closer to understanding an elusive creator. "My religion," he said, "consists of a humble admiration of the illimitable superior spirit who reveals himself in the slight details we are able to perceive with our frail and feeble mind."[1]

In fact, much of his scientific curiosity seemed driven by a desire to understand the superior mind of God. "I want to know how God created this world. I am not interested in this or that phenomenon, in the spectrum of this or that element. I want to know His thoughts, the rest are details," he said.[2]

What Einstein never grasped is that God *has* revealed many of His thoughts in the Scriptures, which make it clear that God isn't interested in our reducing Him to a neat list of equations and theories. His desire is for His created beings to know and love Him.

Without that understanding, it's not surprising that Einstein's optimism about the advancement of mankind

cooled toward the end of his life. After urging President
Roosevelt to support the development of nuclear energy, he
became increasingly convinced that man would soon use
atomic weapons to destroy the world. In 1946 he wrote a
public letter to the United Nations supporting a one-world
government. In 1955, the year he died, he helped draft the
Russell-Einstein Manifesto, which urged all governments to
abolish war. The alternative, the document warned, was
certain destruction.

Without a God who cares about this world, there is no
hope. That is not surprising. Reading the paper or watching
the news often sets us back on our heels. The human capacity
for violence stuns us; countries making selfish and often
stupid decisions affect the lives of millions.

A few hundred years before Einstein grappled with the
apparent hopelessness of the nuclear age, a religious belief
called Deism flourished. Many of America's founding fathers,
including George Washington, Benjamin Franklin, and
Thomas Jefferson, joined its ranks. But Deism, despite its
famous followers, is inherently flawed. Like Einstein, Deists
believed that the knowledge of God comes through the rational mind alone, not through revelation. While it is true that
we can glean some truth about God through rational thought,
it is far from adequate. We need revelation. Deists also
believed that God created the universe, kick-started it in
motion, and then took a few steps back to see how things
would turn out. They believed God is more observer than
participant in His own creation.

If we believe that God has set His gearbox in neutral, then
the whole discussion of His will is immaterial. If He is unin-
volved, then His will is without function in our world and
lives. Believers know better. Instead of being aloof, God is
active in history and with individuals. From the first words in
Genesis to the last words in Revelation, we see a God not
"way out there somewhere," but "right here, right now." We
know from the testimony of the Bible, of history, and of our
own experiences that God is involved in His creation.

Furthermore, contrary to the thinking of Einstein and the

Deists, God has a plan for this earth. More than that, He has a will that will bring it to pass. True, we are not privy to all the details. But just as the simplicity of a diamond is made stunning by the complexity of its angled cuts, so God's will is compelling in part because of its nuances.

G. Campbell Morgan said, "There is no phrase more often in use in Christian thought and speech than that of 'The Will of God.' It constantly recurs in our reading of Scripture; our hymns are very many of them concerned with it; and in prayer we give utterance to it again and again."[3]

Some of God's will is done by Him and Him alone. Creation, for example, is the result of God's applied will. Likewise, human existence came about by God exercising His will. God needed no help in these areas, required no additional guidance or support. It is what He desired; it became what it is.

Only God could make a universe. Only God could populate the place we call Earth. Only God could formulate a redemption plan that would enable Him to be faithful both to His love and to His justice. Only God can see the future.

In the highlands of Peru are some unusual lines that have captured the attention of the world. Ancient peoples created geometric shapes and stylized drawings of birds and other wildlife on the rocky Nazca plain. At ground level, the images are impossible to make out, but from the air, they seem to come to life. Discerning God's overall will is much the same as looking at this artwork from ground level. Our view is limited and therefore so is our understanding. If we could see things from God's perspective, the puzzles of life would make more sense.

Time is linear, at least for humans. Yesterday, today, and tomorrow always follow in procession. That order is never changed. The cosmos has a beginning and it will also have an end. We can plan for tomorrow; work for tomorrow; but we can never know tomorrow. God can, and He has plans for the future.

The scholar Ralph Martin calls these plans the "invincible will."[4] God has a plan and that plan is well underway. His will is indomitable and unalterable. Fourteen hundred years before Christ, the Pharaoh of Egypt resisted the direct will of God when Moses ordered him to free God's people. It went badly for the king.

From the time that Abel offered a worthy sacrifice, God's people have demonstrated a desire to know and follow God's will. As Bernard Edinger said, "Inside the will of God there is no failure. Outside the will of God there is no success."

In Old Testament times, the great men and women of God looked forward to what is now our history. They had questions that remained unanswered. We speak of the Cross, the Resurrection, the church, salvation by grace, and a hundred other topics in the past tense. That means we stand at an enviable point in history.

GOD'S WILL UNREVEALED

Abraham, David, Isaiah, and their contemporaries had to look to a time yet to be and imagine what God might be doing to provide salvation for His people. Some gazed ahead with great clarity. Job, a man who lived in the age of the patriarchs, said, "As for me, I know that my Redeemer lives, and at the last He will take His stand on the earth" (Job 19:25). Living as much as two thousand years before Christ, this afflicted man speaks of a living Redeemer who will stand on the earth. How much did he know? Did he have details about the manner in which Christ would come, the reception He would receive, the disciples He would make? Did Job know that the Redeemer would die for his and the world's sins, only to be raised from the dead and ascend into heaven? Probably not. He did know, however, that God had a plan and a Redeemer in mind. The details would come twenty centuries later.

God commanded the great patriarch and the father of Jewish people, Abraham, to sacrifice his son Isaac on an altar at a place God would show him. Abraham, heartbroken over the demand that would cost him his son, traveled to the chosen place, ascended a mountain, prepared an altar, and laid a knife to his only son's throat. The passage in Genesis 22 tells us the angel of the Lord stopped the proceedings before any harm came to Isaac. Reading the chapter infuriates many, and it should. It's supposed to upset us. We ask, "How could God require such a thing from a father?" Only when we realize that Abraham was acting out in human terms what God Himself had to do, do we understand the point. There was no one to stop God from sacrificing His only Son for us.

When Abraham was moving up the hill, Isaac said, "Behold, the fire and the wood, but where is the lamb for the burnt offering?" (v. 7). How hard it would have been to answer that question, but Abraham did so in an unexpected way. Abraham said, "God will provide for Himself the lamb for the burnt offering, my son" (v. 8). How much did the great man know? Did he understand that God would really do to His own Son what He was asking Abraham to do? Could he have pictured Jesus being beaten and then driven through the crowded streets to the cross on which He would die? Abraham couldn't have known what we now know.

In addition to prophecy and stunning examples of fore-shadowing, God sometimes seemed to use odd means to communicate His will during the Old Testament period. Two objects are mentioned several times. They appeared over four thousand years ago and still have scholars scratching their heads. They were mysterious, powerful, and a little eerie. The Urim and Thummim appear without explanation and disappear in the same way. Bible students speculate about their substance, power, and nature, and when all is said and done, we know little more than when we began. What we do know is fascinating. With them, people spoke to God, and God revealed His will.

It is possible that *Urim* comes from a Hebrew word meaning "Lights," while *Thummim* means "Perfections." "Lights and Perfections"–great names for these bizarre items. They first appeared in the days of Moses, and they did so without introduction or explanation, as though they had dropped out of heaven (see Exodus 28:30). Centuries later, they disappeared. No one knows where or how. We do know that they were kept with the breastpiece of the high priest and were used only on rare occasions.

What did they do?

They revealed the mind of God. Through the Urim and Thummim a person, usually the high priest, could ask God a question and receive an answer. King David used them to determine battle decisions. In one case when he asked whether to pursue an army, he was told, "Pursue, for you will surely overtake them, and you will surely rescue all" (1 Samuel 30:8). That was a very specific answer.

Today we wonder how they worked. The ancient body of Jewish writing called the Talmud teaches that the stones flashed letters that the user could read. Some think that they were stones that were tossed like dice to reveal yes and no answers, but that is unlikely since the answers are never a mere yes or no. The ancient historian Josephus said that the stones would glow in God's presence.[5] Whatever way they worked, God spoke through them. In a sense, they were divine communication devices.

At times we might wish we had access to a device like the Urim and Thummim that would tell us exactly what God is thinking and wants from us. Yet the fact is that we have something better: God's own insights into His plan for all times.

We look back; the people of the Old Testament looked ahead. We have details; they had promise. The mystery of God's will has been laid before us. It was His plan from the beginning. The plan is not new; God had it in mind all along. A simple survey of the phrase "foundation of the world" yields remarkable insight to God's plan. Jesus tells us that a kingdom has been "prepared for you from the foundation of the world" (Matthew 25:34). This kingdom was not an afterthought; it was part of the original plan. In the High Priestly prayer found in John 17, Jesus remarks that the Father has loved Him from "before the foundation of the world" (John 17:24). The list goes on: He has chosen us "in Him before the foundation of the world, that we would be holy and blameless before Him" (Ephesians 1:4). Peter states that Jesus "was foreknown before the foundation of the world" (1 Peter 1:20).

A single word sums up God's will for humankind: relationship. The biblical word is reconciliation. As a divorced husband and wife might reconcile to restore the marriage, so God's overall will is that the sin that separates us from Him be erased and that we return to our original relationship. Everything centers on that understanding.

THE GOD WHO REVEALS HIMSELF

Paul expresses this truth in a letter he wrote to the church in the beautiful and important harbor town of Ephesus. From the first few verses, Paul lets the readers know that God has let them in on information that was unknown to their forefathers: "He made known to us the mystery of His will" (Ephesians 1:9).

In this verse Paul uses the Greek work *thelematos,* translated "will." The same word appears about fifty times in the New Testament and consistently means desire, purpose, and intent. It is the heart of God's desire, that which either is or which He wishes to see take place.

Paul reminds his audience that God revealed one part of the mystery when He sent Christ. The Messiah looked and acted much different from what the Jews expected. Though He came quietly and His ministry was brief, Jesus turned the universe upside down. The details are common knowledge to us, but Paul didn't want us to forget that this was the point when God "broke in" to human history and unveiled the mystery of reconciliation.

As Christians, we know the story of Christ's passion so well that we often forget how unexpected and dramatic God's plan for redemption was. In his book *Mere Christianity,* C. S. Lewis described God's faithfulness: "Though our feelings come and go, His love for us does not. It is not wearied by our sins, or our indifference; and, therefore, it is quite relentless in its determination that we shall be cured of those sins, at whatever cost to us, at whatever cost to Him."[6]

And the modern reader gets a fresh perspective on this truth when reading Lewis's children's series, *The Chronicles of Narnia.* The second book in the series, *The Lion, the Witch and the Wardrobe,* centers on Aslan, a magnificent lion and benevolent ruler of the land of Narnia, and several children who magically enter this kingdom and meet him there. Narnia is engaged in a battle between good and evil, with the White Witch seeking the destruction of Aslan and his followers. The climax of the book comes with Aslan's willingness to lay down his life to spare the life of Edmund, one of the children who has been tricked by the witch into following her. Aslan knows that the White Witch has claim to any traitor to himself or the great Emperor-Over-the-Sea. Remarkably, to spare Edmund's life, Aslan offers his own.

"A howl and a gibber of dismay" rise up when the evil White Witch and her followers see Aslan walking sadly but purposely toward them to sacrifice himself.[7] Clearly, Aslan remains in control. As soon as they discover Aslan won't resist them, the evil beings tie him, muzzle him, and shave him before the witch, cackling with pleasure, slays him with a knife on the Stone Table. Hours after the witch declares victory, however, Aslan comes back to life.

After joyfully embracing him, Lucy and Susan, the two young children who witnessed his death and heard the Stone Table crack when he came back to life, ask him what it all means. "When a willing victim who had committed no treachery was killed in a traitor's stead, the Table would crack and Death itself would start working backwards," writes Lewis.[8] It sounds like a modern retelling of Christ's passion, doesn't it?

Amazing as Jesus' death and resurrection are, Ephesians 1:10 reveals that God's will is not completely done: there is more to the story. God has plans for the future. Paul tells us that God has made known the mystery of His will based on His kind intention "with a view to an administration suitable to the fullness of the times" (Ephesians 1:10).[9]

When speaking of God's will, Paul uses a word translated as *administration* in the New American Standard Bible. The root word means "house" and refers to someone responsible for the activities of a large home. In a sense, the word means "management." God is time's manager. We are subject to time. No matter how hard we try, we can never keep tomorrow from following today or unwinding yesterday. God has no such limitations. Instead of limitations, He has unlimited possibilities.

Now here is the good part: He has made some of that knowledge available to us. He has unveiled a bit of the playbook. He tells us that the Kingdom that Christ came to earth to reveal will be fully realized in "the summing up of all things in Christ, things in the heavens and things on the earth" (v. 10). That is the mystery: the thing formerly hidden but now revealed. While we may not know all the details of how God will bring all things under Christ, we have been given enough information to keep our minds busy for a lifetime. Even better, we're assured in verse 11 that God "works all things after the counsel of His will." In other words, we know the ending, and it's a good one!

God is the great Administrator. Amazingly, He has given us a part to play. Timothy George noted, "The Christian faith has a purpose and a goal and is going somewhere. Unlike many religions and popular philosophies today, Christians do not see the world as a great wheel swirling endlessly around and around in cyclical repetitions that go on forever. No, Christians believe that the world, and everyone in it, has a special destiny, a rendezvous with eternity for which our life on earth is but a preparation."[10]

HIS WILL, OUR WILL

When Christians speak of wanting to find God's will today, often they mean God's will for *them*. Before considering how to determine God's will for us as individuals, it is helpful to understand the role of the will in our own lives and how it intersects with God's. Every being (including the Creator) has three qualities that define the nature of his or her being: intellect, emotion, and will. Intellect is the ability to think; emotion the power to feel; and will the gift of being able to choose. We share those attributes with God. They compose a portion of what it means to be created in His image. It is an honor to share such traits; it is also a problem. Being able to think, feel, and make decisions frees us to live the life for which God created us, but it is those very qualities that drive a wedge between the Almighty and us.

Since the fall of Adam, we have been a stubborn people, self-willed. By nature, we desire to exert our will on God rather than seek His will for us. He made us to be thinking, decision-making people. God designed humans to have freedom of choice even though that meant that many would reject Him. It's an odd situation. In order to make us creatures who could see, feel, love, and serve, God had to risk losing us to our own selfish wills.

Here is the will of God for us: that we *choose* Him. The two greatest gifts from God are forever tied together: salvation and choice. Choice is a liberating power. It can unleash the best in us, but it can also lead us from where we should be. Parents with a teenage driver in the home know the unsettling feeling that overshadows them when their child is out with the car. This fear has two origins: love and memory. First is love. Parents worry over their children. There is no way around it; it is the price of love. Second is the all too vivid memory of being a teenager intoxicated with the new power of driving. Often our own past comes back to haunt us. As parents, we work hard to rear our children to be sensible and independent. But when they begin to exercise that independence, we become nervous, knowing that our children do not always make the right decisions.

God has empowered us and freed us to live our lives. That is a gift of love. Just as we desire that our children listen to our hard-earned wisdom, so God requires that we listen to Him. To do so is to make our wills subservient to His greater will. Our Western culture teaches us otherwise. We are a freedom-loving people and anything that smacks of subservience tastes bad. As C. S. Lewis said, "There are only two kinds of people in the end: those who say to God, 'Thy will be done,' and those to whom God says, in the end, 'Thy will be done.'"[11]

How can we overcome our natural desire to follow our own wills? The apostle Paul writes, "Therefore I urge you, brethren, by the mercies of God, to present your bodies a living and holy sacrifice, acceptable to God, which is your spiritual service of worship. And do not be conformed to this world, but be transformed by the renewing of your mind, so that you may prove what the will of God is, that which is good and acceptable and perfect" (Romans 12:1-2).

His words are urgent and his tone serious. Again, we are back to choice. We can present ourselves to God or to the world. We may choose to conform our minds to this world or have them transformed by God. Giving our minds, hearts, and souls to God for "improvement" opens vast, new realms of possibility. It is also the only way to prove what the will of God is.

JESUS, OUR EXAMPLE

Jesus Himself stressed the importance of knowing the will of God. He said, "For whoever does the will of God, he is My brother and sister and mother" (Mark 3:35). Note the emphasis on doing—doing implies knowledge of what needs to be done. It was important enough for Jesus to make it part of the Lord's Prayer: "Your kingdom come. Your will be done, on earth as it is in heaven" (Matthew 6:10). The Lord's Prayer is a guide for all prayer. At the heart of that petition, Jesus teaches believers to seek the *doing* of God's will on earth as it is *done* in heaven.

In fact, the greatest advice on godly living comes from Christ, and He—the King of kings, Messiah, Anointed One, God's only begotten Son—placed Himself under the will of God. A brief survey of His words shows how completely He surrendered to His Father's will.

- "I can do nothing on My own initiative. As I hear, I judge; and My judgment is just, because I do not seek My own will, but the will of Him who sent Me" (John 5:30).
- "For I have come down from heaven, not to do My own will, but the will of Him who sent Me" (John 6:38).
- "My food is to do the will of Him who sent Me and to accomplish His work" (John 4:34).

Even more striking than Christ's words are His actions of obedience, particularly on a dark night in a place called "Oil

Press," better known as the Garden of Gethsemane. Scores of paintings have been done by artists attempting to capture what must have been the loneliest, most grueling and emotional time any person has endured. Jesus, face down on the ground in prayer, utters heartrending words that threaten to shred the soul of any who imagine it. Jesus was not just sad, He was "grieved and distressed" (Matthew 26:37). By His own admission, He was "deeply grieved, to the point of death" (Matthew 26:38). This was no mere depression, it was not simple anxiety, it wasn't even abject fear; it was the weight of the world on His shoulders. So He prayed and prayed hard. And what words did He use? "My Father, if it is possible, let this cup pass from Me; yet not as I will, but as You will" (Matthew 26:39).

These now famous words represent the only time when the will of Jesus differed at all from the will of His Father. In those dark hours while Judas the traitor was striking his deal, while weary disciples dozed nearby, Jesus surrendered the natural desire of self-preservation to the more difficult will of God. We are the beneficiaries of that love and dedication. Jesus set aside the human desire to avoid the Cross to come and embrace death for our sakes, and it was all in accordance with the will of God. Jesus never asks of us anything more than He asked of Himself.

In fact, it is only because Jesus chose to follow His Father's will rather than His own that we can seek to find God's personal will for us now. Only when we were reconciled with God through Christ did the revealed will of God become personalized. Only then could we understand God's specific and individual will for us.

One of the great realizations about the mystery of God's will is that we're part of it and an important part at that. Many Bible verses illustrate how people can meet the desires of God. Money for the impoverished believers in Jerusalem was given by the Christians of Macedonia "by the will of God" (2 Corinthians 8:3-5); slaves were to live out their servitude "doing the will of God from the heart" (Ephesians 6:5-6); the faithful were to "rejoice always; pray without ceasing; in everything give thanks" because that was "God's will for you in Christ Jesus" (1 Thessalonians 5:16-18). The list goes on.

As Christ demonstrated, being obedient to God's will isn't always easy. The great apostle Peter wrote the book of 1 Peter to Christians who had been scattered abroad by persecution. Most had lost everything they owned. He comforted them in an unexpected way. Instead of saying, "There, there, it's all going to be fine," he encouraged them to look past the moment and see the greater glory. "Therefore, those also who suffer according to the will of God shall entrust their souls to a faithful Creator in doing what is right" (1 Peter 4:19). Suffer according to the will of God? It doesn't seem right, does it? Faithful people in a cruel world who suffer day after day for no crime that they committed, and Peter sees it as God's will! Peter was very familiar with Someone Else who suffered according to God's will. In fact, he was an eyewitness to it.

Faith is a pattern of living. It has as its goal obedience to God through Jesus Christ, with an eye toward Christ's assured victory over the forces of darkness. Before doing God's will, we must immerse ourselves in His thinking. That changes everything. The apostle John wrote, "The world and its desires pass away, but the man who does the will of God lives forever" (1 John 2:17, NIV). Lives forever! No small statement there. God's will changes everything.

God's will was so entrenched in the mind of the apostle Paul that he used the phrase "Paul, an apostle of Christ Jesus by the will of God"[12] to begin most of his letters, which are now included in the New Testament. Paul could not see himself apart from God's will, nor should we.

Each day is a new opportunity to seek the will of God, a new opportunity to demonstrate to the world that a relationship with our Maker through Christ is wise, necessary, and transforming. The mystery of God's will is the revelation of His personal involvement in the life of humanity and each individual who makes up humanity.

When we honor Christ by doing God's will, the world often can't help but notice. Martin and Gracia Burnham served as missionaries in the Philippines for over fifteen years. In May

2001, they were kidnapped while celebrating their wedding anniversary at an island resort. For over a year they wandered aimlessly through the Philippine jungle with their captors, members of an Islamic terrorist group called the Abu Sayyaf who wanted a large ransom in exchange for their release. A harrowing part of their experience was enduring numerous gun battles between the Philippine military, who were trying to free the hostages, and the Abu Sayyaf. Despite their hunger, fear, and humiliation, Martin and Gracia spent hours reminding one another of God's faithfulness and trying to demonstrate God's love to their captors.

June 7, 2002, began like any other day in captivity. After many hours of marching, it began to rain and the small group stopped hiking. The Burnhams were allowed to rest. As they set up their hammock, Martin told Gracia, "I've been thinking a lot lately about Psalm 100–what it says about serving the Lord with gladness. . . . We may not leave this jungle alive, but we can leave this world serving the Lord 'with gladness'; we can 'come before his presence with singing.'"

Minutes later, just after they had settled into their hammock for a nap, gunfire erupted. The Philippine army was making another rescue attempt. This time, Martin was killed; Gracia was shot in the leg–so no happy ending followed a seemingly wasted year in the jungle.[13] And yet, the Burnhams' story has made many people wonder: How could two people, treated like animals for months, display such love toward their captors? How could they hang on to hope?

Perhaps A. W. Tozer sums it up best: "When the eyes of the soul looking out meet the eyes of God looking in, heaven has begun right here on this earth."[14] Even in excruciating circumstances Martin and Gracia did not stop seeking God and His will, giving observers a glimpse of God's kingdom.

The greatest miracle of all is that God chooses to be a part of our lives–every day. What remains is our choosing to be a part of His life by choosing His will. And the surest way of doing that is by following Christ, the greatest mystery revealed by God.

FOR REFLECTION

1. What evidence do you see that God is involved and interested in His creation? Why is it important to acknowledge this before we seek to determine His will?

2. What advantages do we have in knowing and following God's will as compared to those who followed God during the Old Testament period?

3. The Bible tells us that God's will, His plan for us, has been in place "from the foundation of the world." What are some of the truths about God and His plan that have been in place from the beginning of time? (See Matthew 25:34; John 17:24; Ephesians 1:4; and 1 Peter 1:20.)

4. How would you define God's will?

5. How do you react when you discover that your will and God's will for you are not the same? See Romans 12:1-2 for some advice from Paul.

6. Describe the internal struggle Christ had in the garden of Gethsemane as He sought to follow the Father's will over His own.

CHAPTER 3

Jesus: The Mega Mystery

Child of Bethlehem, what contrasts you embrace! . . . We come in hushed reverence to find you as God, and you welcome us as man. We come unthinkingly to find you as man, and are blinded by the light of your Godhead.

EPHRAEM THE SYRIAN, A FOURTH-CENTURY WRITER

By common confession, great is the mystery of godliness: He who was revealed in the flesh, was vindicated in the Spirit, seen by angels, proclaimed among the nations, believed on in the world, taken up in glory. 1 TIMOTHY 3:16

I CONFESS. I'm spoiled. On my computer are not one, but three Bible study programs–the high-end ones. I can search scores of translations, tap into some of the best commentaries and language tools, and much more. On my bookshelves are a few hundred books including commentaries, devotionals, and theology texts. In my e-mail, I get net newsletters from *Christianity Today, Leadership, Pastors Today*, and others. Via the Internet, I can access sermons and theological works as well as other helpful resources. It's all here at my fingertips.

I'm not the only "spoiled" modern Christian. Most Christian homes have many Bibles in different translations. It's hard for us–it's hard for me–to imagine those early days of the church when a single copy of the Old Testament could cost a year's wages. Imagine spending this year's salary to buy a Bible.

How did the early Christians learn God's word? They listened. They memorized. And they sang. Hymns, songs, and confessions became memory aids. Paul told the church in Ephesus that they should "[speak] to one another in psalms and hymns and spiritual songs, singing and making melody with your heart to the Lord" (Ephesians 5:19).

A hymn is a spiritual teaching set to music. Many of the hymns we sing today carry a message meant more to inspire than instruct. First-century Christians often sang Scriptures set to music or hymns that taught doctrine. It was an effective way to remember important and fundamental beliefs.

Paul included one such song in his letter to a young pastor named Timothy. Tucked away in that little book are six lines from an early doctrinal song: "By common confession, great is the mystery of godliness: He who was revealed in the flesh, was vindicated in the Spirit, seen by angels, proclaimed among the nations, believed on in the world, taken up in glory." In those short verses is the phrase "mystery of godliness"–another secret revealed.

Could you sum up the life of Christ in a handful of words? It seems a daunting task, especially since God inspired the writing of four separate Gospels to get the important information across to generations of believers. Even John, the author of one of those Gospels, conveyed his frustration when he concluded, "And there are also many other things which Jesus did, which if they were written in detail, I suppose that even the world itself would not contain the books that would be written" (John 21:25). When all is said and done, there is still more to be said and done.

Still, teaching the basics to tens of thousands of new believers was important and challenging work in an age that couldn't conceive of photocopy machines or Sunday school literature. Teachers taught doctrine orally and Christians committed everything to memory. Paul told Timothy to remember to teach a common confession, something Timothy recognized. He learned it from Paul and he shared it with his own congregation.

That spiritual ditty–short as it is–reveals a great deal about Jesus. In a sense, those short lines are a summary of what was taught in those early days of the church. By no means was the early Christian's knowledge limited to these few lines, but the words would call to mind much of what they had already learned. It was a spiritual mnemonic intended to

assist believers' memories, one that still reminds us of the
greatest of all mysteries—Jesus the Christ.

THE GREATEST MYSTERY OF ALL

"By common confession," Paul writes in 1 Timothy 3:16. The
word translated *confession* comes from the Greek term
homologoumenos, meaning to "speak the same thing." It
means to be of the same saying, that is, to hold the same
belief. Many denominations have a formal document called a
confession of faith, a summary of the organization's beliefs.
These confessions or creeds are a digest of doctrine.

What Paul relates, the church held as indisputable truth.
And what a truth it is. Paul says, "Great is the mystery of
godliness." In this instance, he uses the word *mega* for
"great." The apostle calls this a "mega mystery." Christ is
certainly that and more. Of all the mysteries we'll cover in
this book, none can eclipse Jesus. We've seen that a mystery
is something formerly hidden but now revealed. Jesus fits
that description perfectly. In fact, He is the living definition of
the term. Even now, in the twenty-first century, we can
scarcely take in what we know of Jesus.

During my first pastorate, we held a ceremony honoring a
retired minister, who was also the founder of our church. We
respected him for his keen insights into the Bible. During the
service, I had him stand. I said, "Brother, you've served the
Lord and taught the lessons of the Bible as an ordained
minister for sixty years now. Have you learned it all?"

The honoree laughed, shook his head, and said, "No, I'm
just getting started." It's hard to believe that a man who had
served the Lord for six decades could feel that he was just
getting started on his understanding of the Bible.

Learning about Christ is like dipping water out of the ocean
one coffee cupful at a time. We could remove enough water
to last us a lifetime and the ocean wouldn't know the difference. The depth and breadth of Christ defies a complete
understanding, but we can still know a great deal. That's
what makes it such a grand adventure.

It was in Antioch that believers were first called Christians.[1] When the term was used by non-Christians, it usually wasn't meant as a compliment. But for the believer it was an accolade. We can say nothing better of a person than that he or she belongs to Christ, displaying in daily life the eternal truths of the Savior. Jesus is not an abstract idea, not a philosophy to debate in the halls of universities and seminaries. While the study of His life is the highest pursuit anyone can undertake, such activities are useless unless we forge a relationship in the furnace of belief.

Jesus is the center and breadth of all. He is the object of faith, the instrument of our salvation, the conduit of communication with the Almighty. Without Him, we are mere shells of life; with Him, we are the children of God. Blaise Pascal lived fewer than forty years, yet his influence on the world continues 380 years later. Noted for his work as a philosopher, mathematician, and physicist, the Frenchman had one of the finest minds the world has known. Interestingly, the world remembers him for his defense of the faith more than any other accomplishment. He said of Jesus, "Not only do we not know God except through Jesus Christ; we do not even know ourselves except through Jesus Christ."

Pascal—who at the age of sixteen formulated Pascal's theorem, a foundational concept in geometry; who invented the first mechanical adding machine; and who made many other significant scientific observations—found the study and service of Christ to be the greatest of all human endeavors. He understood that Jesus is the greatest mystery ever revealed.

It is this idea that the early church made into a formal confession. It is the importance, supremacy, and centrality of Christ that compelled Paul to call to mind the ancient confession. What a glorious mega mystery Christ is.

"REVEALED IN THE FLESH"

The first element in the common confession found in 1 Timothy 3:16 is that Jesus was "revealed in the flesh." Usually when we read the word *reveal* in our English Bibles, it is the translation of a Greek word that means "to unveil." Here, however, a different word is used (*phaneroo*), a word that is often translated as "manifested." It means to make visible something unseen. In this case, Jesus came in the flesh.

That's no small statement. The Incarnation ("in the flesh") is a crucial doctrine of the faith but one that stretches even the most elastic minds. "Jesus Christ is God in the form of man; as completely God as if he were not man; as completely man as if he were not God." Those are the words of A. J. F. Behrends, a nineteenth-century pastor. Such things are easy to say but often difficult to grasp. How does God dwell in human form?

No human (apart from Christ) will ever be wiser than King Solomon. He did not earn his wisdom by life experience. It was a supernatural gift from God. Solomon built the great Temple and dedicated it to God. At the Temple's dedication, the great man knelt in prayer, raised his hands to heaven in typical Jewish style, and said, "But will God indeed dwell with mankind on the earth? Behold, heaven and the highest heaven cannot contain You; how much less this house which I have built" (2 Chronicles 6:18). Solomon summed up the problem: How does an infinite God fit in a finite space? The Temple was a large structure but by no means enormous. Nonetheless, it was much larger than a grown man, and it could not hold the essence of God.

The wildly popular book *The Da Vinci Code* suggests that the early church did not believe that Jesus was truly God. The author is wrong; the incarnation of Christ is a biblical fact. A brief survey of the New Testament reveals that it was a doctrine held from the very beginning. In his Gospel, John wrote, "And the Word became flesh, and dwelt among us, and we saw His glory, glory as of the only begotten from the Father, full of grace and truth" (John 1:14). Christ's coming in the flesh was part of the plan from the very beginning. Intent is the key. Christ did not arrive by accident; He came *on* purpose and *with* purpose. By choice, He became flesh; by choice, He dwelt (literally, "took up residence") among other physical creatures; by choice, He was seen and displayed glory, grace, and truth. This was so important to John, he began his Gospel narrative emphasizing Jesus' appearance in the flesh and also wrote in his first letter:

> *We proclaim to you the one who existed from the beginning, whom we have heard and seen. We saw him with our own eyes and touched him with our own hands. He is the Word of life. This one who is life itself was revealed to us, and we have seen him. And now we testify and proclaim to you that he is the one who is eternal life. He was with the Father, and then he was revealed to us. We proclaim to you what we ourselves have actually seen and heard so that you may have fellowship with us. And our fellowship is with the Father and with his Son, Jesus Christ. (1 John 1:1-3, NLT)*

Paul added, "But when the fullness of the time came, God sent forth His Son, born of a woman, born under the Law, so that He might redeem those who were under the Law, that we might receive the adoption as sons" (Galatians 4:4-5). Again, we can't help noticing the intention, planning, and implementation.

For ten years, I made my living as an architectural project manager. Every day I would go into the office and spend hours drawing lines on paper, rendering in two dimensions what I was envisioning in three. There were three exciting moments in those days: (1) when I began a new project, (2) when I finished a project, and (3) when I visited the finished building and could walk through what had formerly only been an image in my mind.

Architects may draw impressive plans, beautiful in scope, punctilious in detail, but they are little more than graphite on paper if the building never rises above the ground. The plans of God are not theoretical, not abstract, and certainly not wishful thinking. He formulated them in His mind to achieve a purpose, to reach a goal, to bring us back into fellowship with Him. Jesus came in the flesh as an infant and adopted us into His family.

The Incarnation required a sacrifice on Christ's part. "Have this attitude in yourselves which was also in Christ Jesus, who, although He existed in the form of God, did not regard equality with God a thing to be grasped, but emptied Himself, taking the form of a bond-servant, and being made in the likeness of men" (Philippians 2:5-7). What must it have been like to leave behind the glories of heaven for life on earth with all its limitations and pains? We know what it is like to visit a beautiful place, to find exceptional comfort, enjoy unimagined peace, and then have to leave to return to the everyday world of traffic, taxes, bills, and work. Yet Jesus left so much more, and He did so knowing the rejection, the hatred, the trials, the beatings, and the Cross that awaited Him. Only love of the highest order could compel someone to do that.

Taking on the physical was a necessary part of the plan. In John 4, Jesus met a Samaritan woman at a well. A discussion ensued. That alone was shocking. A first-century Jewish rabbi just did not carry on a conversation with a Samaritan woman. After some back and forth about where people should worship, Jesus laid it on the line. "God is spirit, and those who worship Him must worship in spirit and truth" (John 4:24). Yet there Jesus stood in the flesh. Jesus confined Himself to the body of a human male. We should be careful here. Jesus did not adopt a body for a time only to dispose of it later. Jesus went to the cross in His body, was buried in His body, was raised from the dead in the same body, and ascended into heaven with that body now glorified.

Paul spoke of the day when he would see Christ face-to-face and Jesus would put a "crown of righteousness" on his head, something He does for every believer (see 2 Timothy 4:8). The day Paul was beheaded in Rome, he stood before the Savior he had served so faithfully in life and received a much-deserved crown. But what did Paul see? A ghost? An angel? No, he saw the resurrected Savior, nail prints still in His hands. Jesus retains His body forever, just as resurrected believers will theirs.

Jesus needed to be human to go to the Cross and to experience death on our behalf. The Resurrection demanded a body. We have a Redeemer whom we *could* relate to, but also one we *can* relate to. Beautiful, powerful present tense: Jesus was; Jesus is; Jesus shall forever be!

Every year, Christmas cards fly through the postal system. Upon opening the envelopes, we discover images of angels, manger scenes, and the like decorating the front of the card. Inside are sweet Christmas wishes. The world loves Christmas but often overlooks the big picture. Celebrating the Incarnation is good. Remembering that its goal was our salvation is crucial. From a stone manger to a stone tomb, that was the meaning of the Incarnation for Christ.

Philip Yancey says it well. "As a Christian I believe that we live in parallel worlds. One world consists of hills and lakes and barns and politicians and shepherds watching their flocks by night. The other consists of angels and sinister forces and somewhere out there places called heaven and hell. One night in the cold, in the dark, among the wrinkled hills of Bethlehem, those two worlds came together at a dramatic point of intersection. God, who knows no before or after, entered time and space. God, who knows no boundaries took on the shocking confines of a baby's skin, the ominous restraints of mortality."[2]

The mega mystery of Christ is the irreconcilable idea that God became man so that man could meet God.

"VINDICATED IN THE SPIRIT"

Part of the commonly held confession of those first Christians was that Jesus was "vindicated." It seems an odd term to use in relation to Christ. We believe Him to be sinless, perfect in every way. In what way did He need vindication? Quite simply, it had to be shown that the man Jesus, who was crucified in such a degrading manner, was the Son of God.

The key to understanding the 1 Timothy 3:16 passage is to take note of its structure. There are six lines to the stanza; three pairs with words in opposition. For example, in this couplet "Spirit" stands in contrast to "flesh." Jesus came in the flesh, but He was not universally received as God. His critics were many and vocal. Even His disciples struggled with the concept. Jesus told Philip, "He who has seen Me has seen the Father" (John 14:9), and Philip didn't get it.

During His ministry, Christ's humanity could be seen clearly, but during two events the world caught sight of the divine Jesus. The first was on the Mount of Transfiguration; the second was the Resurrection.

Jesus took on flesh for many reasons, but the chief one was the Cross and the Resurrection. An occupied tomb meant failure; an empty sepulcher meant success not just for Jesus but also for all believers.

The mechanism of the Resurrection is unknown. No one this side of heaven can formulate a comprehensive list of steps taken by God to raise His only begotten Son. The apostle Paul, however, does comment, "But if the Spirit of Him who raised Jesus from the dead dwells in you, He who raised Christ Jesus from the dead will also give life to your mortal bodies through His Spirit who dwells in you" (Romans 8:11). While we can't list the steps taken by God, we do know that His Spirit was the agent in the Resurrection and will be so in ours as well. This is the manner in which Christ was "vindicated." On several occasions, He foretold His death and resurrection but each announcement fell on confused or embittered minds. On the third day after His death and interment, Jesus was vindicated by stepping into the spring sunrise as alive as anyone has ever been. The world has been taking notice ever since.

Then as now, Christians needed to know that the Incarnation was just the beginning. The death and Resurrection were the high mark of all that Jesus came to do. The Resurrection remains proof that Jesus was everything He claimed to be. It is the linchpin of the Christian faith.

"Christ Himself," the great theologian B. B. Warfield said, "deliberately staked His whole claim to the credit of men upon His resurrection. When asked for a sign, He pointed to this sign as His single and sufficient credential." Warfield was referring to a response Jesus made when the Pharisees and scribes demanded a show, a miracle from the Savior. "An evil and adulterous generation craves for a sign; and yet no sign will be given to it but the sign of Jonah the prophet; for just as Jonah was three days and three nights in the belly of the sea monster, so will the Son of Man be three days and three nights in the heart of the earth" (Matthew 12:39-40).

We can imagine the looks of disdain on the faces of the critics. No one had ever made such a claim. It was one thing to predict one's demise and even manner of death. It is quite another to predict a personal resurrection and the day it will occur. After the event, people could claim that a suicidal Jesus choreographed His own demise, but they couldn't wave off the Resurrection.

Occasionally, police officers face the difficult situation of a distraught man with a gun who threatens them in hopes that the police will kill him. They call it "suicide by cop." The perpetrator wants to die but for some reason can't commit suicide, so he hopes the police will end his life. Jesus never gave any indication that He looked forward to death. The garden of Gethsemane argues against such an idea. He was *willing* to go to the Cross so that He could lay down His life for His friends. Still, some might argue that the Cross was the result of a clever scheme orchestrated by Jesus. But how does someone orchestrate His own resurrection? He can't.

The moment Jesus stepped out of the cold tomb He authenticated everything He had taught. It had always been true, but the Resurrection made it unmistakable and irrefutable. That is why so many of His enemies tried to disprove the Resurrection. If it weren't important, they would have simply shrugged and said, "So what?"

Jesus came in the flesh, died in the flesh, and was raised in the flesh. That is a key element in the mega mystery of Christ. And still there is more.

"SEEN BY ANGELS"

Mentioned over three hundred times in the Bible, angels have become one of society's favorite subjects. Angel art, angel statues, angel earrings, and angel television shows can be seen everywhere. Yet angels—at least biblical angels—remain mysterious. Books have been written, verses compiled, and studies made, but when all is said and done we are left with only a vague understanding of these intelligent creatures. Although mentioned in thirty-four books of the Bible, no one is able to prove their existence. The Bible writers, however, make no apology for the many times angels are mentioned, assuming their existence as a fact. Angels appear and disappear at will to carry messages, do battle, and observe humankind. Angels announced Christ's birth and ministered to Him after the temptations in the wilderness and after His agony in the Garden of Gethsemane. Angels were present at His Resurrection and Ascension.

So what are they? In short, they are created, sentient beings with abilities superior to humans. Most serve at God's behest, but some rebelled and God cast them from heaven. Angels are also involved in the worship of God. A full study of angels requires more space than allowed here, but it is important to note that the early church's doctrine included the fact that Jesus was "seen by angels." But what angels?

The mind runs to heavenly beings. It's a natural assumption. Philippians 2:9-11 teaches, "For this reason also, God highly exalted Him, and bestowed on Him the name which is above every name, so that at the name of Jesus every knee will bow, of those who are in heaven and on earth and under the earth, and that every tongue will confess that Jesus Christ is Lord, to the glory of God the Father." Even those in heaven will bow their knee. From that we learn two things: One, intelligent beings populate heaven and, two, they worship Christ.

But there's another possibility. The ancient confessional song may not mean angels as we understand them. *Angel* means messenger. The term makes no distinction between human messengers and heavenly ones. I believe that if the confession follows a logical sequence, then Christ was "revealed in the flesh," (Incarnation), "vindicated in the Spirit," (Resurrection), and then "seen by messengers" (witnesses to the resurrected Christ).

The number of witnesses to the resurrected Jesus numbers over five hundred, according to 1 Corinthians 15:6. Over forty days, Jesus appeared a recorded twelve times and in a variety of places and situations. The first to see Jesus after the Resurrection were Mary Magdalene and a group of women (Luke 24:10). Mary Magdalene had the honor of being the first to deliver the message of the empty tomb. Others would see and believe. These became messengers of the truth; witnesses to the greatest historical event ever.

One of the enduring mysteries of Christ is His deposit of trust in frail, sometimes frightened people to carry the eternity-altering news of Christ to the world. The message wasn't given to the intellectual elite, the wealthy, the established religious leaders, or the people of power. It was given to those women and men who were untrained in teaching technique, communications skills, marketing, and publicity, and it tipped the world on its side.

Which is it? Heavenly angels? Human messengers? Since both are true, it doesn't matter. In light of what comes next, I believe that the confession likely refers to the human witnesses, but angels were present at the Resurrection and witnessed the actual event, something no human can say.

"PROCLAIMED AMONG NATIONS"

What does one do with a message like the Resurrection? Such news is hard to sit on, especially if you've been an eyewitness. Making the matter even more urgent is Christ's command to tell the world. We saw earlier that Acts 1:8 records the direct, personal commissioning of the disciples. "But you will receive power when the Holy Spirit has come upon you; and you shall be My witnesses both in Jerusalem, and in all Judea and Samaria, and even to the remotest part of the earth."

First, Jesus promises His disciples that they will receive power. The power would come upon them in the form of the Holy Spirit and they were to appropriate that power. This power would enable them to fulfill the assignment Jesus gave them. And what was that assignment? It was rather unique. Often we read this verse and assume that Jesus is telling them to go into the world near and far and start preaching sermons. In a sense, that is true, but Jesus didn't call them to be evangelists; He called them to be witnesses. Witnesses are people who give an account of what they have personally seen or experienced. They do not give hearsay evidence, but testimony. By sharing what they knew to be true as witnesses, the early Christians became evangelists, missionaries, teachers, and apostles.

Witness is a legal term hammered to shape a new meaning. Originally, the term referred to someone who spoke from personal experience, but opposition to the gospel gave it new meaning. The Greek word for witness is *martus.* It may look familiar. Our word *martyr* comes from it. Today we know a martyr to be someone who dies because of his or her faith. The first Christian witness who died for his faith was a deacon named Stephen. Ironically, one of the people present at his stoning was Saul of Tarsus, a man now known as Paul the apostle. In recounting some of his early life, Paul confessed to his preconversion sins: "They themselves understand that in one synagogue after another I used to imprison and beat those who believed in You. And when the blood of Your witness Stephen was being shed, I also was standing by approving, and watching out for the coats of those who were slaying him" (Acts 22:19-20). Paul met Jesus in a dramatic encounter while he was traveling to Damascus to persecute believers. Ironically, Saul the Christian persecutor became Paul the persecuted. He became a witness and his witness eventually made him a martyr. But because of his faithfulness, the Word went out and continues to change lives today.

Matthew records another commissioning passage. Often called the Great Commission, it outlines not only the mission but also the goal. "And Jesus came up and spoke to them, saying, 'All authority has been given to Me in heaven and on earth. Go therefore and make disciples of all the nations, baptizing them in the name of the Father and the Son and the Holy Spirit, teaching them to observe all that I commanded you; and lo, I am with you always, even to the end of the age'" (Matthew 28:18-20).

Ask most Christians, "What is the most important task of

the church?" and the reply will be, "Evangelism." It is a good answer, and while it's not wrong, it isn't quite correct. Jesus gives only one verb in this passage, followed by three participles: going, baptizing, and teaching. The command is to make disciples. Disciple-making involves not only evangelism but also education and guidance. It is never enough to lead someone through the sinner's prayer. At that point, a convert is made but not a disciple. *Disciple* refers to someone who has become the student of another. Evangelism is one component of disciple-making. It is the point of beginning but not the end.

The confessional song cited by Paul reminded the believer that the message of Jesus was global. Jesus never traveled out of His country, yet every country today has a Christian witness because those early believers took seriously the disciple-making command of Christ. Witnesses went out proclaiming the message; people believed and aligned with the church.

This proclamation was to the nations (*ethnos*, from which we get our word *ethnic*). The message of Christ began with Israel but He meant it for the whole world. In Jesus' day, the Temple area had been expanded until it covered over thirty acres. The complex consisted of the main building, ancillary structures, and courtyards. The largest courtyard was for the Gentiles. Surrounding the main Temple area was the Wall of Sanctuary that delineated the "Jews only" area from the Gentile court. In 1871, a limestone block was discovered in Jerusalem. The block measured twenty-two inches by thirty-three inches and had inscribed on its face:

NO STRANGER IS TO ENTER WITHIN THE BALUSTRADE
AROUND THE TEMPLE AND ENCLOSURE:
WHOEVER IS CAUGHT WILL BE RESPONSIBLE TO HIMSELF
FOR HIS DEATH, WHICH WILL ENSUE.

It was a grave warning that the Jews took seriously, as Paul learned.[5] In many ways, Jesus unwound the old system. Instead of keeping Gentiles out, He welcomed them into His church and not passively–He sent His disciples to the

Gentiles. His was an aggressive outreach that continues today.

"BELIEVED ON IN THE WORLD"

Wherever witnesses share the message of Christ, people respond in faith. Some, perhaps most, will reject the truth, but there are always those who believe. That's the power of Christ. *Believe* is a powerful word. The term Paul uses means to realize that something is true, but it also carries the idea of acting on that belief. It's not simple belief in which a truth is recognized, but a truth that compels a commitment. This belief touches every part of a person: mind, heart, and soul.

The apostle James penned one of the most shocking verses in the Bible. "You believe that God is one. You do well; the demons also believe, and shudder" (James 2:19). It's an eye-opener. Even Satan believes in God, yet his belief is without commitment, service, love, or relationship. Belief is more than mental assent; it is the depositing of our life in God through Christ. Belief is not just held, it is used. Belief changes the believer.

Throughout the world, there are those who believe. We can't help noticing once again that there is a global aspect to this statement. Paul wrote and the early Christians recited, "Believed on in the world." In this context, the Greek word, translated as "world," refers to the populated areas of the globe. The idea is profoundly simple and profoundly amazing: God shares His love with all who believe. That doesn't sound impressive in the twenty-first century—although it should. We've been hearing words like this for two thousand years. We can become calloused to it. That is why the Bible presents it as a mystery, something formerly hidden and now open to all.

Unlike the Temple complex with its compartmentalized courts for Gentiles, women, and priests, the church has no such barriers; it makes no such distinctions. It was not exaggeration when Jesus said, "For God so loved the world, that He gave His only begotten Son, that whoever believes in Him shall not perish, but have eternal life. For God did not send the Son into the world to judge the world, but that the world might be saved through Him" (John 3:16-17). From the beginning, Jesus had His eyes set on people everywhere.

"TAKEN UP IN GLORY"

Before a stunned group of disciples, Jesus issued the final lesson of His earthly ministry by charging them to go and make other disciples. Then He was lifted up into the air, disappearing into a cloud. What a sight it must have been. But where did Jesus go? Where is He now?

Eric Reed of *Leadership* magazine tells of a woman who approached her pastor after one Easter service. "So what happened with Jesus after the Resurrection?" she asked. "Well, He ascended into heaven and He's still alive," the pastor answered. "I know He was resurrected, but He's *alive?*" The pastor assured the woman that was the case. "Alive?" the woman said. "Alive? Why didn't you tell me?" Reed says the woman telephoned everyone she knew to exclaim, "Jesus is alive! Did you know He's alive?"[4]

The Ascension ended one ministry for Jesus but began another. Jesus did not retire after the Resurrection. His work continues. He ascended bodily to glory where He "sat down at the right hand of God" (Mark 16:19; see also Romans 8:34). His earthly work is finished so He sits in the prominent place, but His relational work achieved by the Cross and Resurrection continues.

So what is Jesus doing? No list could encompass all that He does, but the Bible does shed some light on His present activities.

Christ is interceding for His people. "Therefore He is able also to save forever those who draw near to God through Him, since He always lives to make intercession for them" (Hebrews 7:25). Jesus is the conduit, the avenue of prayer. We pray in His name for good reason—He intercedes for us. *Intercede* means to speak on someone else's behalf, to plead their case, even to mediate in a dispute. Jesus is our intercessor. The author of Hebrews states, "He always lives to make intercession." Nothing will change the work of Christ. We have an intercessor who speaks up for us, who makes it possible to maintain our relationship with God.

In a similar way, Jesus is also our Advocate. An advocate is a legal representative. Jesus is our "legal counsel" in heaven. "My little children," John says, "I am writing these things to you so that you may not sin. And if anyone sins, we have an Advocate with the Father, Jesus Christ the righteous" (1 John 2:1). John uses the same word that Jesus did to describe the Holy Spirit–*paraklete*. The word appears only five times in the New Testament, and Jesus uttered four of those. In each of those cases in the *New American Standard Bible*, the word translates as "Helper." The meaning of the term is "one called alongside." It can mean comforter, aide, and encourager. The Holy Spirit is our Comforter on earth, but Jesus is our Helper before God. What better representative can we ask for than the sinless Savior?

Jesus also aids the church. It makes sense that since Jesus founded the church and shed His blood for her He naturally continues to watch over her. Jesus "nourishes and cherishes" the church "because we are members of His body" (Ephesians 5:29-30).

He also indwells the individual members of the church. Paul spoke of being "crucified with Christ" and that "Christ lives in me" (Galatians 2:20). The purpose of that indwelling is that we can live to and for God. That's a difficult task. Sin shackles us and trips us up. We all need help to be obedient. Christ is there not only to be our Advocate when we sin, but also to help us overcome sin. Again, the author of Hebrews hits the nail on the head: "For since He Himself was tempted in that which He has suffered, He is able to come to the aid of those who are tempted" (Hebrews 2:18).

The early Christians recited a confessional song that reminded them of Jesus' present-day, ongoing work. It is a work we should remember, too.

THE CLEAREST MYSTERY OF ALL
It is hard to comprehend all that Christ did and is doing. It is difficult to take in His nature, sacrifice, love, power, and dedi-

cation to the individual and the church. Scholarly books try to do so but the heart of a poet is needed.

Christ remains the clearest mystery of all. Although millions of pages have been written about Him, although heated theological debates have raged, the simple truth is still the best truth: Jesus came, died, was resurrected, was seen by witnesses, and ascended into heaven where He cares for those called by His name.

FOR REFLECTION

1. How was the doctrinal confession found in 1 Timothy 3:16 used by the early church?
2. Identify the segments of the mega mystery of Christ.
3. Each segment of this mystery is awesome. Which part stands out as most significant to you?
4. If a nonbeliever asked you what makes Jesus so significant to Christianity, how would you respond?
5. Besides what Christ did for us here on earth, what is He doing for believers now?

PART TWO

The Mystery of the Kingdom of God

CHAPTER 4

The Kingdom of God and of Heaven

The only significance of life consists in helping to establish the kingdom of God. LEO TOLSTOY

Now having been questioned by the Pharisees as to when the kingdom of God was coming, He answered them and said, "The kingdom of God is not coming with signs to be observed; nor will they say, 'Look, here it is!' or, 'There it is!' For behold, the kingdom of God is in your midst." LUKE 17:20-21

ONE Sunday, while practicing my usual routine of wandering the worship center to greet as many people as time allowed before the service began, I came to a young man sitting with his head down, his eyes fixed on something before him. I soon learned it wasn't his Bible. Instead, he held an electronic device–a handheld computer. I asked what model he had and he proudly told me that his was no ordinary handheld computer. His was fully equipped with GPS software. GPS–Global Positioning System–that amazing bit of techno-magic that allows a person to determine where on Earth's 197 million square miles he is. The device could pinpoint his position within 100 feet. Sure enough, he was in the right church. Of course, he didn't need twenty-four satellites hovering 12,500 miles above the Earth's surface to tell him that.

GPS systems are in our cars, carried in our pockets, used to track delivery trucks and monitor military troops. For some people, knowing where they are is crucial. As believers, though, we often are so caught up in the details and circumstances of our physical location that we don't stop to consider our spiritual position. When we do try to pinpoint where we are spiritually, we tend to do so based on the kind of church we attend.

We further define ourselves by our denomination: Baptist, Episcopal, Lutheran, and even "nondenominational." We like pigeonholes. It gives us a way of defining our beliefs and ourselves. Among serious Bible students and scholars, these definitions reach an almost extreme level. "I'm a premil, pretrib, dispensationalist, and a two-and-a-half point Calvinist," I've heard people say. It sounds like a pedigree. Such designations are convenient handles in some circles, but they sometimes overshadow the simplicity of who we are in Christ. While it is good to have a well-delineated doctrine, it is also important to remember that it matters more *whose* we are than *who* we are.

Where are you? Not physically, but spiritually. Can we have a spiritual position as real as our physical one? Yes, we can, and the place we are is the Kingdom of God.

THE KINGDOM IDEA

For most of us, kingdoms are outdated—items in history books or lessons from high school. Several kingdoms still exist in the twenty-first century, but their numbers are few and many no longer resemble their glorious past. In the West, democracy has replaced many or turned thrones into symbols instead of unquestioned authority. Only one kingdom remains unchanged since its founding. It is the oldest kingdom in the world—and beyond the world.

The Kingdom of God is a reality little known to many Christians. The term is often used, but the practical understanding goes unnoticed. We speak of Jesus being King of kings; we sing praise hymns like "All Hail King Jesus," without giving thought to what the words mean. Yet Jesus often spoke of the Kingdom of God—as much a reality to be experienced now as a place to be anticipated at Christ's second coming.

Christianity is not a democracy, it is instead a theocracy—a government ruled by God. It is a true monarchy. Unlike a democracy in which the citizens decide their leaders by vote, God was, is, and will always remain King over the universe. While He gives us great latitude in the conduct of our lives, the operation of our churches, and our daily decisions, God remains the ultimate authority for His people.

It might seem confusing to speak of both God the Father and His Son, Jesus, as kings, but such is the case. Paul wrote Timothy encouraging him to be patient for the return of Christ that would only occur in God's timing, "which [God] will bring about at the proper time—He who is the blessed and only Sovereign, the King of kings and Lord of lords" (1 Timothy 6:15). Paul saw God as the true King. John referred to Jesus by the same titles: "These will wage war against the Lamb, and the Lamb will overcome them, because He is Lord of lords and King of kings, and those who are with Him are the called and chosen and faithful" (Revelation 17:14). In a sense, God's government is a coregency.

From the time of their deliverance from Egypt until they pleaded for an earthly king, the Hebrews maintained a true theocracy, a government directly led by God. But they longed for a human king and pleaded with the prophet Samuel to intercede before God on their behalf. Samuel resisted but God gave him instruction to follow the people's request. The Lord's words carry a sense of sadness and profound disappointment: "Listen to the voice of the people in regard to all that they say to you, for they have not rejected you, but they have rejected Me from being king over them" (1 Samuel 8:7).

This was the end of true theocracy for the Hebrews, but not the end of the Kingdom of God. No human or human institution can dethrone the Almighty. He remains in charge.

Kingdom thinking was still part of first-century Jewish thought. A Gentile king, a Caesar sitting in Rome, ruled them, and it was something no Jew stomached easily. Their hunger was for the Messiah to come and free them from such bondage, and return the nation to its spiritual roots and its glory days. Jesus came prepared to do just that—but not according to their script. Because He didn't resemble the Messiah they'd been expecting, many Jews rejected the true King to continue in bondage.

When the Pharisees asked for more details, even a timetable, of the coming of God's Kingdom Jesus replied that the

kingdom of God was already in their midst, but in an unexpected form. It was not accompanied by the signs and
outward display that the Pharisees expected and without
which they would not have been satisfied.[1]

Not only would Jesus not give them the signs they
demanded, His values were directly opposed to theirs, as the
Beatitudes in Matthew 5 made clear. Instead of pride, Jesus
advocated spiritual poverty; instead of power, gentleness;
instead of riches, righteousness; instead of personal comfort,
commitment to God's Kingdom.

In fact, the kingship of Jesus put Him on the cross. His
enemies' charge was, "He claimed to be a king." The Roman
guards who tortured Jesus mocked Him, "Hail, King of the
Jews!" and struck Him repeatedly. Pilate asked, "Shall I crucify your King?" only to hear "We have no king but Caesar!"
(John 19:15). And as Jesus hung on the cross, a placard that
read "Jesus the Nazarene, the King of the Jews" was placed
above His head. Kings traditionally go into battle with their
troops: it is rare for a king to insist on fighting the battle alone.

Matthew uses the phrase *kingdom of God* in a parable that
Jesus used to foretell His death. Jesus describes a landowner
who invests his time and money in a vineyard, building a wall,
a tower, and planting vines. He then rents out the vineyard as
was often done in those days. His rent is a portion of the
produce, but when he sends his servants to retrieve what is
rightly his, the tenants beat, stone, and kill the men. He sends a
larger group who meet the same fate. Finally, believing that the
renters will certainly respect his family, he sends his own son.
They kill him. Jesus stood toe-to-toe with those who would
orchestrate His death and told them He knew of their inten-
tions. He then dropped a spiritual bomb: "Therefore I say to
you, the kingdom of God will be taken away from you and
given to a people, producing the fruit of it" (Matthew 21:43).

Taken away? God had entrusted the Kingdom to the nation
of Israel and they were–in the form of their religious leaders–rejecting it. Like the renters, they had come to love what
they had more than the One who gave it to them. Because of
that, God would give the Kingdom to others.

But to whom? It went to the followers of Christ, regardless of their past, their heritage, or their depth of understanding. Christ wanted the unwanted.

The Gospels' first mention of God's Kingdom centers around the fiery prophet and cousin of Jesus: "Now in those days John the Baptist came, preaching in the wilderness of Judea, saying, 'Repent, for the kingdom of heaven is at hand'" (Matthew 3:1-2). John the Baptist was not an easy man to overlook. He came out of the wilderness like a storm. He was thunder wrapped in flesh, and when he preached he did so in a pointed way certain to hit home. His message was not a feel-good mantra. He called the Pharisees and the Sadducees a "brood of vipers" (Matthew 3:7). Unkind words about the unkindest of men. The religious leaders saw themselves as upstanding examples of religious discipline, but John the Baptist saw them as a wriggling, squirming pit of snakes.

John used inflammatory rhetoric in his sermons. "The axe is already laid at the root of the trees; therefore every tree that does not bear good fruit is cut down and thrown into the fire" (Matthew 3:10). Axes could trim branches or—as in this image—destroy the tree. A man who took an ax to the root was a man who wanted to kill the tree. How ironic, that the religious leaders looked for that Messiah who would put to death the overbearing Roman authorities only to hear that it was they who were facing judgment.

"His winnowing fork is in His hand," John proclaimed, "and He will thoroughly clear His threshing floor; and He will gather His wheat into the barn, but He will burn up the chaff with unquenchable fire" (Matthew 3:12). Again, another illustration as harsh as it was unexpected. Central to John's message was the coming Kingdom.

That Jesus would usher in that Kingdom is clear, but what does that mean? What is the Kingdom of God?

A KINGDOM MIND

How interesting that we preach and discuss the Kingdom so little. It is our home; the place we will spend eternity.

Although we have yet to see the future aspect of the Kingdom that comes with Christ's return, we have seen and know enough to appreciate that God's Kingdom exceeds all others. Someplace along the line, the church has lost its Kingdom view. The first word out of John the Baptist's mouth was that the Kingdom of God was at hand. Jesus echoed those words early in His ministry and continued to teach the Kingdom as one of the great mysteries of God.

The New Testament mentions the Kingdom of God nearly seventy times and that number climbs to over a hundred when we count Matthew's thirty-plus references of the Kingdom of Heaven. (The terms are largely synonymous.) That's approximately the same number of times the word *church* appears and more times than *forgiveness* or *saved*. Still, we seldom mention Kingdom concepts in our churches. Most Christians do not speak of their membership in the Kingdom or include it in their thinking.

Kingdom preaching was at the core of the early church. Jesus "presented Himself alive after His suffering, by many convincing proofs, appearing to them over a period of forty days and speaking of the things concerning the kingdom of God" (Acts 1:3). The core of Jesus' post-Resurrection appearances revolved around the announcement of the Kingdom. We see that in the early sermons of his followers. Philip preached "the good news about the kingdom of God and the name of Jesus Christ" (Acts 8:12). The topic was at the heart of Paul's teaching: "And he entered the synagogue and continued speaking out boldly for three months, reasoning and persuading them about the kingdom of God" (Acts 19:8).

"But seek first His kingdom and His righteousness, and all these things will be added to you" (Matthew 6:33). The words come as a command—an imperative, not a suggestion. There are many good things to seek, but the Kingdom should be at top of the list.

The Kingdom is everywhere. It has "offices" in every country, among people of every language, and includes people of every economic strata. Borders cannot define it. Surveyors cannot mark its corners. Its volume is beyond measure; its members are greater than the sum of their parts. It issues no passports, has no immigration authorities, and holds no elections. Geography cannot describe it, philosophy cannot define it, and time cannot contain it. We are subjects in a Kingdom whose population includes the living and those who have died; a monarchy overseen by a benevolent King who values His subjects more than His citizens value themselves.

The Kingdom is not a "someday" thing. There will be a time when the Kingdom of God and Christ will be easily seen; a time when Christ rules on earth and all things are under His control, but the Kingdom is now. Our feet walk the streets of where we live, but our hearts and souls know that they also walk the streets of a Kingdom that is not of this world.

Summing up the transcendence of the Kingdom, pastor and author John Piper says:

> *This is the mystery (the secret) of the kingdom—the arrival of the kingdom in a preliminary, small way in advance of the final consummation when all the enemies would be defeated and all sin and satanic power and sickness and suffering would be gone forever.... Fulfillment of the kingdom is here; consummation of the kingdom is not.[2]*

It is only when we see the Kingdom that we truly see God as Father and Christ as King. It is an insight that compels us to realize that we are part of something far greater than any earthly kingdom or empire; that we have a citizenship that goes beyond the country of our birth. This understanding changes our view of ourselves and our obedience to God.

A PLACE FOR THE USED-TO-BE

As a young pastor, I once received an envelope in the mail unlike any I had ever received. Not long before, I had baptized a woman. She was a middle-aged, married woman with a newfound love for Christ. Prior to baptism, she had started coming to worship services and Bible studies. She was well liked and a pleasure to be around. That made the contents of the envelope even more shocking. As I held the letter in my hand, I noticed the address was scribbled in an awkward hand as if someone was attempting to disguise his or her handwriting. The letter was short: "Is this the kind of person you want in your church?" With the letter were photocopies of photos. The pictures showed a naked woman–the woman I had just baptized. The photos were not lewd or pornographic. It seems she liked to do housework without the distraction of clothing.

I was angry. I was beyond angry. Not at the woman but at the person who sent the letter. Of course, the letter was unsigned. Such cowardice seldom wants attention. I struggled with what to do with the situation. Should I talk to the new Christian? Should I play private detective and track down the nameless writer? I decided against both. The next Sunday, I stood in the pulpit and offered a cryptic communication: "To the person who sent me the unsigned letter, the answer to your question is, yes."

I had no interest in what the woman used to do. Clocks don't run backward. I was interested in what she was becoming in Christ. That is the nature of the Kingdom; it is filled with people who used-to-be.

In another confrontation with the religious leaders, Jesus makes this point with a very short story. "But what do you think? A man had two sons, and he came to the first and said, 'Son, go work today in the vineyard.' And he answered, 'I will not'; but afterward he regretted it and went. The man came to the second and said the same thing; and he answered, 'I will, sir'; but he did not go. Which of the two did the will of his father? They said, 'The first.' Jesus said to them, 'Truly I say to you that the tax collectors and prostitutes will get into the kingdom of God before you'" (Matthew 21:28-31).

These words were as sharp as they could be and must have cut deep into the Pharisees' pride. Jesus made it clear that there was more to faith than keeping laws. Jesus did not call people to be obedient to laws but to the Lawgiver. Everything in Christ's message revolved around the relationship between man and God. The Pharisees and those like them hung their faith on what they did, who they were, and the laws they kept. Jesus taught that God has as much interest in the outcast as He does the socially acceptable. To hear that prostitutes and tax collectors would see the Kingdom of God before the Pharisees was earthshaking. They needed the earth shaken.

A KINGDOM BIRTH

Not all Pharisees were enemies of Christ. Nicodemus approached Jesus with a compliment and got a puzzling statement in return. In fact, the Gospel writer John mentions the "Kingdom of God" in only two verses. They appear in this story.[5] Here's how the Bible records it:

> *Now there was a man of the Pharisees, named Nicodemus, a ruler of the Jews; this man came to Jesus by night and said to Him, "Rabbi, we know that You have come from God as a teacher; for no one can do these signs that You do unless God is with him." Jesus answered and said to him, "Truly, truly, I say to you, unless one is born again he cannot see the kingdom of God." Nicodemus said to Him, "How can a man be born when he is old? He cannot enter a second time into his mother's womb and be born, can he?" Jesus answered, "Truly, truly, I say to you, unless one is born of water and the Spirit he cannot enter into the kingdom of God."*
> *(John 3:1-5)*

Jesus clearly states that there is only one way into the Kingdom, and that's by a new birth. Generally a person becomes a citizen of a country simply by being born to parents who are citizens of the land. Here, Jesus speaks to a Pharisee who was steeped in the Jewish idea that any descendent of Abraham stood in a special place with God. Now the Pharisee suddenly learns that his physical birth was not enough, there had to be a spiritual birth.

No one is in the Kingdom of God by virtue of physical birth. We make a decision in which the grace of Christ is accepted. That is when life begins. R. C. Sproul writes: "God just doesn't throw a life preserver to a drowning person. He goes to the bottom of the sea, and pulls a corpse from the bottom of the sea, takes him up on the bank, breathes into him the breath of life and makes him alive. That's what the Bible says happens in your salvation."[4] It's a vivid picture.

Kingdom life begins with a new birth. It is something we cannot do for ourselves, but which God is willing to do for us. That new birth changes everything. We no longer think the same; our values are different; and most of all we develop Kingdom thinking.

Many times, I have been asked, "How do I know if I'm saved?" The answer I give has two short parts: "Can you remember a time when you asked Christ to be your Lord and Savior?" I want to know if there was a purposeful, decision-making event. Then I ask, "Are you any different since that time?" I don't ask if they're perfect. The answer to that is clear. We're all sinners. What I want to know is if they have changed. The Bible tells us that "if anyone is in Christ, he is a new creature; the old things passed away; behold, new things have come" (2 Corinthians 5:17). With new birth comes new attitudes, new desires, and new allegiances. Nicodemus would go on to defend Christ before other Pharisees (see John 7:50-51) and would become a very public disciple by tending to Jesus' lifeless body after the crucifixion (see John 19:38-40).

With that new birth comes new citizenship in the Kingdom of God–a Kingdom where God rules not just in the world but also in the heart. In short: We are not *born* into the Kingdom; we are *reborn* into it.

"For the kingdom of God does not consist in words but in power" (1 Corinthians 4:20), Paul told the believers in Corinth at a time when they were struggling with false teaching. It is the power of Christ to change lives; power that Jesus' critics refused to see.

Paul wrote to the very troubled church at Corinth, a church that had every possible sin associated with it. Paul had to deal with the problem of temple prostitutes, incest, sexual immorality, false teaching, homosexuality, and more.

He wrote, "Or do you not know that the unrighteous will not inherit the kingdom of God? Do not be deceived; neither fornicators, nor idolaters, nor adulterers, nor effeminate, nor homosexuals, nor thieves, nor the covetous, nor drunkards, nor revilers, nor swindlers, will inherit the kingdom of God. Such were some of you; but you were washed, but you were sanctified, but you were justified in the name of the Lord Jesus Christ and in the Spirit of our God" (1 Corinthians 6:9-11).

Sadly, there are those who wield this verse like a club inflicting harm rather than attracting the spiritually hungry. So sharp are the sins that it is hard to notice the grace. Fornications, idolatries, adulteries, effeminate (male prostitution), homosexuality, thievery, drunkenness, swindlers, and more are impossible to ignore. The dull hammer blow of "will not inherit the kingdom of God" accompanies those edgy sins. Then the sentence that is so often overlooked appears, "Such were some of you."

There in that first-century congregation were adulterers, homosexuals, idol worshippers, and more. They formed the ranks of the great class of Used-to-Be. Christ changed them. Their entrance into the Kingdom came with washing, sanctification, and justification. The freshly born Christians, along with every other believer, composed the citizenry of the Kingdom, proof that the Kingdom of God cares nothing for the way things were but cares everything about what is and is to be.

Former drunks, drug addicts, thieves, lying politicians, cheating preachers, and just plain ol' sinners walk the streets of God's Kingdom. In the Kingdom, what matters is what Christ has made of us. We surrender the former lifestyle gladly to seize something far better. Paul's other point is that those who continue to practice such things are not part of the Kingdom, whether now or in the age to come. As Paul put it, "For He rescued us from the domain of darkness, and transferred us to the kingdom of His beloved Son, in whom we have redemption, the forgiveness of sins" (Colossians 1:13-14).

LET US SPEAK OF KINGDOM THINGS

Malcolm Muggeridge literally traveled the globe seeking
another kingdom. This first-rate journalist quickly became
disillusioned with the political systems he observed and
wrote about in England and India. As a young man, he realized his greatest hope—communism—was a sham less than a
year after being assigned as a correspondent in the Soviet
Union. His insightful reporting on the unchecked famine
created by Stalin, who let his own people starve in an attempt
to centralize all agriculture, was quickly denounced by
others, including George Bernard Shaw.

Though it would be another fifty years before he accepted
the claims of Christ, Muggeridge became something of a
prophet, warning against the dangers of becoming too
comfortable in this world. "The only ultimate disaster that
can befall us . . ." he said, "is to feel ourselves at home here
on earth."[5]

He warned his readers about the deadening effects of mate-
rialism and the false "freedom" granted by such things as
abortion; yet at the same time, he wrote movingly of the
earth's beauty and the solace that could be found in another's
love.

Still Muggeridge continued his search for another kingdom.
Long before joining the church, Muggeridge was a great
admirer of Mother Teresa—in fact, he was the one to first
bring her to the world's attention with his 1971 book *Something Beautiful for God*. She once told him: "You are to me
like Nicodemus. . . . I am sure you will understand everything
beautifully if you would only become a little child in God's
hands."[6]

After he and his wife joined the Catholic church in 1982, he
wrote of the deep peace he finally felt: "a sense of homecom-
ing, of picking up the threads of a lost life, of responding to a
bell that had long been ringing, of taking a place at a table
that had long been vacant."[7]

Muggeridge lived with his feet firmly planted in this world,
yet he always seemed to have his ear cocked to the faint yet
incessant calls from a distant Kingdom. He wrote persua-

sively about the shortfalls of earthly systems yet found no peace until he cast his lot with that unseen Kingdom, the one created by God Himself for His own people.

Kingdom people, those who proudly count themselves among the Used-to-Be, live fully in this world yet give their first allegiance to the Kingdom of God. This Kingdom is every Christian's country, worthy of our patriotism, respect, dedication, and service. It is more than a philosophical construct, more than a theological badminton game. It speaks to who we are, Whom we serve, why we live, and is a goal far greater than human imagination can make or fully comprehend.

And, perhaps, it is the source of our noblest longings and purest hopes. As Frederick Buechner writes: "If we only had eyes to see and ears to hear and wits to understand, we would know that the Kingdom of God in the sense of holiness, goodness, beauty is as close as breathing and is crying out to be born both within ourselves and within the world. . . . The Kingdom of God is where we belong. It is home, and whether we realize it or not, I think we are all of us homesick for it."[8]

We are a destination-driven people. When we travel, we focus on where we plan to be and overlook where we are. Like travelers on a train who draw curtains across their windows, we can miss the beauty and blessing of the trip. There will be a time when evil will be no more, when tears will no longer trickle down cheeks, when uncertainty will certainly be an item of history, but our joy and purpose should not be put off to the end. We are Kingdom people. We are subjects of a King who died for His citizens. Christ's throne should be at the center of our hearts and minds, and should be the subject of our sermons, Bible studies, and prayers.

As Christians, our feet walk on foreign soil that has become home for us, but our hearts are in another Kingdom. There is no higher honor or more noble an action than to be a proud member of the Kingdom of God.

FOR REFLECTION

1. Discuss the differences between a theocracy and a democracy.
2. In what ways is the Kingdom that Christ ushered in different from what the Pharisees and many other Jews expected?
3. How does one know if he or she is part of the Kingdom of God?
4. Name some Kingdom priorities. How do your thoughts and actions reflect them?
5. Can you identify with Frederick Buechner's observation that many people are "homesick" for the Kingdom of God? If yes, in what way?

CHAPTER 5

The Perplexity of Parables

I sometimes wonder what hours of prayer and thought lie behind the apparently simple and spontaneous parables of the gospel. J. B. PHILLIPS

I will open my mouth in a parable; I will utter dark sayings of old. PSALM 78:2

All these things Jesus spoke to the crowds in parables, and He did not speak to them without a parable. MATTHEW 13:34

WHEN Jesus spoke about the Kingdom of God, He didn't use cleverly crafted theological platitudes or follow a three-point sermon outline. Instead, He told simple stories.

Storytelling is an ancient practice but it is also a modern art. Where once stories passed from person to person, they now come to us through our television sets, movie theaters, and books. The human mind resonates with story. It is the way God has designed us.

A portion of our brain immediately comes alive when someone starts a tale, joke, or an account. "Story isn't imposed on our lives," says the poet Luci Shaw, "it invites us into its life and as we enter and imaginatively participate, we find ourselves in a more spacious, freer, and more coherent world."[1]

Perhaps that is why the Bible is constructed the way it is, filled with historical events portrayed with drama. Stories, images, metaphors, similes, and allegories fill the Old Testament, and all for a reason: Story communicates spiritual truth in a memorable way. "Story has the power to grasp bits of the past and carry them into the imaginative present, rescuing us from the pitfalls of abstraction," Shaw says.[2] It's one thing to read the statement, "God loves you." It's another to read a story about an elderly man running joyfully to embrace his filthy, smelly son who's slinking home after squandering much of his father's wealth, and then realize Jesus told it to illustrate how much we are loved.

This ability to share a life-changing truth by story reaches its pinnacle in the ministry of Jesus. His sermons, corrections, and teachings were more likely to contain a story than not. It was Jesus' way of revealing spiritual mysteries.

Many of the secrets revealed by Jesus came by way of parable. The word *parable* comes from the New Testament Greek word *parabole* which means "to set side by side"–to compare one thing to another. What Jesus did so brilliantly was to take the new and unfamiliar and dress it in clothing that anyone could recognize. Bible teachers are fond of defining a parable as an earthly story with a heavenly meaning. That's a good description. A parable is a story that uses the familiar to teach the new; to compare a known truth with an unknown truth. In an agricultural society such as the one in which Jesus ministered, stories of fields, plants, animals, farm buildings, and the like were well known. A truth about the Kingdom of God painted on the mind in familiar colors made the truth easy to grasp, simple to remember, and simple to share–at least for those with inquiring hearts.

Others were not receptive. Jesus used parables not only to reveal truth to believers but also to confound His critics. *Perception* is a function of *reception.* It was true then and it's true now. We do not perceive until we first receive.

PAR-"ABLE"—PAR-"INABLE"

When Jesus began His ministry, He taught with such refreshing openness that His audience couldn't help but comment on the authority of His words (see Matthew 7:28-29). Jesus was the Great Communicator, but not everyone liked His sermons. Jealous religious leaders contaminated the crowds that gathered around Jesus. Every time Jesus spoke, He knew there were detractors in the congregation–detractors who would one day drive Him to the Cross.

These critics were more than just cynics. Jesus posed a threat to them, their system, their standing in society, and their comfort. When Jesus spoke plainly, they challenged His words, arguing fine points in an effort to show His teaching as inferior to their own. It never worked. For some people lies are more comfortable than truth.

What Jesus did was pure genius. He began teaching in parables. At first, this was puzzling to the disciples. His hand-picked followers came to Him and asked, "Why do You speak to them in parables?" (Matthew 13:10). The answer was unexpected:

> *To you it has been granted to know the mysteries of the kingdom of heaven, but to them it has not been granted. For whoever has, to him more shall be given, and he will have an abundance; but whoever does not have, even what he has shall be taken away from him. Therefore I speak to them in parables; because while seeing they do not see, and while hearing they do not hear, nor do they understand. (Matthew 13:11-13)*

At this point, we might want to ask, "Why bother teaching at all?" If the purpose of a parable was to keep people from understanding, then why spend time traveling and teaching? In fact, it seems cruel to teach someone who cannot understand. But there is more to this, as we see in the verses that follow. Jesus went on to say:

> *In their case the prophecy of Isaiah is being fulfilled, which says, "You will keep on hearing, but will not understand; you will keep on seeing, but will not perceive; for the heart of this people has become dull, with their ears they scarcely hear, and they have closed their eyes, otherwise they would see with their eyes, hear with their ears, and understand with their heart and return, and I would heal them." But blessed are your eyes, because they see; and your ears, because they hear. For truly I say to you that many prophets and righteous men desired to see*

what you see, and did not see it, and to hear what you
hear, and did not hear it. (Matthew 13:14-17)

For those with open hearts and receptive minds, a parable
becomes a par-"able." Parables require thinking and thinking
takes effort. Those who care enough to want the truth and to
invest thought and discussion in Jesus' words would be able
to get the spiritual points. They would listen. They would
reason. They would get it. There were many of those in the
crowd. For them the parables became open doors to spiritual
knowledge as well as an effective way of sharing the same
message. Preachers know that the illustrations they use in a
sermon long outlive the sermon itself. The same is true with
a parable. We can imagine a person in the crowd going home
and being asked by a neighbor, "So what did the rabbi have
to say?" He could then tell his friend the parable just the way
Jesus had.

There were others in the masses that surrounded Jesus
who had no desire to learn. They felt they knew it all. It was
this group that Isaiah spoke of over 700 years before Christ.
These were the religious leaders—the Pharisees, the Sadducees, and the scribes. The Pharisees were a powerful and
influential group of conservative laymen. They were strict
observers of the Law of Moses and loved ritual. They were
religiously cruel, oppressive, controlling, and impatient with
any who disagreed with them, including Jesus. They were
even willing to set aside their long, hard-fought differences to
join in a conspiracy against the Savior.

The Sadducees were a prominent group that accepted only
the first five books of the Old Testament, the books of Moses,
as being authoritative. They denied the existence of angels or
a physical resurrection. Although they were opponents of the
Pharisees, they did share one thing in common with them—
they despised Jesus.

A third antagonistic group was the scribes. These were
the scholars, the theologians of the day. They held a high
and esteemed place in society, one they relished and were
eager to protect. Jesus taught with greater authority than

they did and the people turned to Him for truth. That did not sit well.

Imagine what it must have been like to travel from town to town followed by a group that included admirers and at least three powerful, influential, well-financed groups of adversaries. They had already begun to level offensive charges at Jesus. Not long into His ministry, Jesus had already been called a lawbreaker for allowing His disciples to pick and eat grain on the Sabbath; been accused of being in league with the devil; been laughed at; and pestered for a miraculous sign and then dismissed because He refused to give them one.[3]

Whenever He spoke to a crowd, Jesus could see the hungry faces of seekers and the scowls of men already committed to destroying Him (see Matthew 12:14). For these onlookers and those like them a parable became a para-"inable." It prevented them from understanding. This might seem the opposite of what Jesus would want, but His enemies were already dedicated to His destruction. What they could not obliterate was the divine teaching. As Isaiah had said seven centuries before, they had let their hearts become dull. Truth was no longer their goal. "To understand and receive the truth is more a matter of the heart than the head," says British pastor, author, and broadcaster Richard Bewes. "The parables were a way of saying, 'How much do you want the kingdom?'"[4]

Of the thirty parables Jesus told, seven of them deal directly with the mystery of the Kingdom of God. These parables made the Kingdom of God an open secret. In chapter 6 we begin with one of the best-known stories that Jesus told.

FOR REFLECTION

1. What is the appeal of parables—both in Jesus' day and in our own?
2. Why did Jesus use stories and parables in His teaching?
3. How does Jesus' teaching style compare with that of pastors and teachers today?
4. Discuss the three types of religious leaders who opposed Jesus' teaching.

CHAPTER 6

Seeds, Dirt, Weeds, and Birds

It takes two to speak the truth—one to speak, the other to hear.

HENRY DAVID THOREAU

That day Jesus went out of the house and was sitting by the sea. And large crowds gathered to Him, so He got into a boat and sat down, and the whole crowd was standing on the beach.

And He spoke many things to them in parables, saying, "Behold, the sower went out to sow; and as he sowed, some seeds fell beside the road, and the birds came and ate them up.

"Others fell on the rocky places, where they did not have

much soil; and immediately they sprang up, because they had no depth of soil.

"But when the sun had risen, they were scorched; and because they had no root, they withered away.

"Others fell among the thorns, and the thorns came up and choked them out.

"And others fell on the good soil and yielded a crop, some a hundredfold, some sixty, and some thirty.

"He who has ears, let him hear. . . ."

"Hear then the parable of the sower.

"When anyone hears the word of the kingdom and does not understand it, the evil one comes and snatches away what has been sown in his heart. This is the one on whom seed was sown beside the road.

"The one on whom seed was sown on the rocky places, this is the man who hears the word and immediately receives it with joy; yet he has no firm root in himself, but is only temporary, and when affliction or persecution arises because of the word, immediately he falls away.

"And the one on whom seed was sown among the thorns, this is the man who hears the word, and the worry of the world and the deceitfulness of wealth choke the word, and it becomes unfruitful.

"And the one on whom seed was sown on the good soil, this is the man who hears the word and understands it; who indeed bears fruit and brings forth, some a hundredfold, some sixty, and some thirty." MATTHEW 13:1-9, 18-23

HERMAN Melville begins his classic fish story, *Moby Dick*, with just three words: "Call me Ishmael." From that sentence on, the reader is in the mind of this character, the novel's narrator and a crewmate of the strange Captain Ahab. The reader sees what Ishmael sees, feels what he feels, and experiences what he experiences.

When we read the events in Jesus' life, we generally use our God-given imagination to place ourselves nearby and mentally watch what He does. We listen to what He says as if He were an actor on a stage. When we read a parable, for instance, we see ourselves in the crowd hanging on every word that Jesus spoke. There is nothing wrong with that, but we often can learn a great deal more if we switch our point of view and try to see the event through the eyes of Jesus.

The crowd has pressed in, Jesus has entered a boat and is afloat a short distance offshore. In the boat with Him are His disciples. The crowd moves to the water's edge. The disciples use the boat's oars to keep the craft in place.

Jesus looks over the water to the mass of people congregating on the shore. What does He see? He sees faces young and old, male and female, all staring at Him. Some smile. Some look puzzled. Some frown with disapproval. They are a mixed lot. Some hunger for the next sermon, others are just curious, some want miracles performed, and others are looking for another reason to hate Him. It is a tough crowd.

In that seaside congregation are Pharisees and other religious leaders who oppose Jesus. Already they have called for miracles on demand, accused Him of breaking the law of Moses and of being in league with the devil. That's what Jesus sees from the boat, an amalgamation of friends and enemies, of the curious and the seekers, of learners and critics.

All of this is important to know before approaching the first Kingdom parable mentioned in Matthew.[1] Jesus is not only being instructive, He's also being corrective. Against this backdrop, Jesus tells the first of seven parables that unveil the mysteries of the Kingdom of Heaven.

BROADCAST QUALITY

The story of the sower is one of the best-known parables in the Bible and yet in some ways it is the least understood. Perhaps this is because so few of us work in agricultural pursuits, and those who do use equipment, tools, and technology far beyond the dreams of farmers in Jesus' day.

Let's take a walk, a stroll back in time. We go to a place where farmers work with crude handmade instruments, not diesel tractors. The society in which Jesus ministered was largely agricultural. Even those who owned businesses or were craftsmen knew the principles of the farm. If we could stand on a farmer's field two thousand years ago, we would see what Jesus describes in this parable. A wide field lies before us; most of the ground is prepared for planting: rocks cleared away, weeds pushed back, the soil flat and ready. Through the middle of the field runs a path of compacted dirt, pressed into place by the feet of the farmer, workers, and people passing through his field. It is hard and sunbaked.

If we look closer, we can see where the field meets the path. Rock and debris line the boundary. By walking around the field, we see that the corners are not as neat as the open area. Along the edge where fertile soil meets wild growth, there are outcroppings of thorny weeds.

Now comes the farmer, perhaps a young man by our calendar but made older by hard work. His face is lined and sun darkened. He walks through the field, near the path. Hanging from his shoulder is a cloth pouch that bulges under the weight of seed, either wheat or barley. He reaches in with one hand, seizes a fistful of seed, and then flings it in an arc in front of him. We call this broadcast planting, because the farmer is casting the seed in a broad pattern before him.

Seeds fly everywhere. They fall on the prepared soil, the path, the rocky ground, and among the weeds. No area is untouched. Then the action begins.

EXTERNAL INTERCEPTIONS

The picture Jesus paints is simple but also unsettling. There is violence in the imagery. Although the disciples needed help in interpreting the parable, it didn't take a theological genius to know that Christ wasn't speaking of grain and lifeless dirt. As always, people were at the heart of the teaching.

The farmer swings his arm and lets fly a handful of seeds into the air. The seeds scatter and fall. Some of it falls on the foot-hardened path. Luke's account adds a phrase missing in the first two Gospels: "and it was trampled under foot" (Luke 8:5). This is harsh imagery—seeds falling to the ground and crushed beneath the feet of unnoticing, distracted travelers. All three synoptic Gospels highlight the coming of birds that eat the seed.

Jesus later explains the imagery. The seeds represent the gospel. Why seeds? Because seeds have life, but only if they are allowed to grow. Seeds in a sack amount to little. By themselves, they are lifeless. Some seeds can sprout after being dormant a few years, others longer. In March of 2002, ABC News reported that Jane Shen-Miller, a plant biologist at the University of California, Los Angeles, had grown plants from seeds that laid dormant in a dry lake bed in China for close to five hundred years.[2]

Some seeds are very durable, but to grow they must be

planted and watered. The gospel seeds in this parable fall on ground hardened by sun and foot traffic. Birds come for a feast, eating all they can find. In His explanation to the disciples, Jesus doesn't speak of birds but of "the evil one." Mark uses the proper name "Satan" (Mark 4:15). Luke uses "the devil" (Luke 8:12). Is there an inaccuracy here? Is it a mistake because each of the three synoptic Gospels uses a different term? No. Each phrase enhances the meaning.

Evil one shows the nature of the act and actor. The word means hurtful, painful, burdensome and, when used to describe a person, can mean wicked. While Matthew's Gospel shows us the nature of the antagonist, Mark's gives us his name: Satan. Satan means "adversary" or "accuser." Both are appropriate. Add Luke's term *devil* and the picture is complete. *Devil* in the original language means "one who slanders." Stitching the accounts together, we get a clear picture of the wicked, slandering adversary who snatches away the gospel "so that they will not believe and be saved" (Luke 8:12).

The natural tendency is to blame the devil for the ineffectiveness of the gospel message, but that would be a mistake. While no one would hold him blameless, the real problem is the soil. Jesus says this soil represents those who hear but do not understand. Understanding means that we are in the idea and the idea is in us. Interestingly, the original Greek word of the New Testament is a compound term combining "send" and "together," meaning to put together. That's the meaning here. When the gospel message goes out, all hear, but not all understand. This isn't to say that the gospel is too difficult to comprehend. Remember this parable isn't about the seeds but about the soils. The gospel is clear enough. The problem rests in the hearer's willingness to understand.

Why would Jesus paint this dismal picture? Remember that He is looking across a short stretch of water at a crowd peppered with His harshest critics. Before explaining His parable, Jesus tells the disciples how blessed they are because their knowledge will increase. But then He quotes Isaiah 6:9–"Go, and tell this people: 'Keep on listening, but do not perceive; keep on looking, but do not understand.'" The Pharisees and other religious leaders had chosen not to believe what they heard and consequently sealed off what they could know. If the heart is locked shut, the mind will refuse to see the truth.

It is no surprise that Jesus says that the evil one snatches away the gospel. Parables are not isolated from the context of society. Jesus told these stories in response to honest questions or vile accusations. After witnessing Jesus casting a demon from a man, the Pharisees said, "This man casts out demons only by Beelzebul the ruler of the demons" (Matthew 12:24). The scribes went even further with a ridiculous accusation that Jesus was "possessed by Beelzebul" (Mark 3:22). In a verbal sleight of hand, Jesus teaches the truth about the coming Kingdom of Heaven while also implying that the scribes and Pharisees were the ones truly in league with the devil.

This is also more than flowery, image-rich speech. According to Mark, the disciples and other followers asked for the explanation to the parable "as soon as He was alone" (Mark 4:10). Mark also notes that all twelve were present for the explanation. Numbered in that crowd was a man named Judas Iscariot. Why bring him up here? Because of a comment Jesus would make at the Last Supper. John 13:27 records that when it came time for Judas to betray Jesus, "Satan then entered into him." There were hard-hearted people who were not Pharisees and scribes. One such person spent three years in Jesus' company and the truth never grew in him.

INTERNAL PROBLEMS

Some plants can grow almost anywhere. We've all seen weeds push through cracks in asphalt or concrete or attempt to take root in a brick wall. Some plants spring from tight fractures in rock faces. Those plants have a hard life and seldom do well. Their growth is stunted, their roots bound, and they are subjected to harsher conditions than they would experience in regular soil. Plants intended as crops, like those described in this parable, cannot endure such conditions.

In the field Jesus describes, the seed planted on rocky soil faces a similar obstacle. Much of Palestine has a limestone pan beneath the topsoil. In some areas, the limestone is near the surface. A seed planted in these regions often leaps to life in the early spring but soon dies because of the rocky layer beneath the roots. As spring days turn hotter, the plant withers, unable to sustain itself because of its anemic root system.

In the Kingdom of God, there are those who take to the gospel message readily, embrace it with joy, but then falter when trouble hits. Like a poorly rooted plant, they wither under extreme conditions. Jesus lists two such situations: affliction and persecution.

Affliction is a sharp and unpleasant word. The original Greek can be translated "anguish." Literally, it means to press together, to put under pressure, to hem in and even to "squash." That's how affliction feels. Today we say, "I feel like I have the weight of the world on my shoulders." It's the same idea, except in this case, someone on the outside is adding to the weight until the afflicted can handle no more.

Jesus compounds the image by also using the word *persecution*. The root word means to flee as if being chased—another uncomfortable picture. Jesus' point is that some will like what they hear in the gospel and will respond, but response is not enough. Associating with the gospel is only a beginning. A good start does not a race make. When pressure, criticism, ridicule, or persecution come because of the gospel, many leave it all behind.

GETTING TO THE PROBLEM OF THE ROOT

Jesus describes such people as having no roots. There is nothing to sustain them when things get hot and, like a plant that can't sink roots deep into the moist, cool soil below, they dry up and the winds of difficulty blow them from the field. Just like sprouts early in the season, it is hard to tell the difference between those whose roots are deep and firm and those with very little root structure.

It may seem strange that those who hear, respond to, and show joy about the gospel message will so easily desert it when the pressure is on. Unfortunately, some seek to attract others to Christianity by promising it as a cure to all problems, the ingredient that makes life fun and trouble free. While there is great joy in faith, the Kingdom of God can be a difficult place to live. The writer of Hebrews pulls no punches in his letter to the early believers:

> *They were stoned, they were sawn in two, they were tempted, they were put to death with the sword; they went about in sheepskins, in goatskins, being destitute, afflicted, ill-treated (men of whom the world was not worthy), wandering in deserts and mountains and caves and holes in the ground. And all these, having gained approval through their faith, did not receive what was promised, because God had provided something better for us, so that apart from us they would not be made perfect. (Hebrews 11:37-40)*

The disciples who heard this parable and received a personal lesson on its meaning would come to understand the price they would pay for their faith. If traditions are correct, only one disciple died a natural death and that was only after years of ill treatment. A brief survey of how the disciples died makes the point.

According to tradition, Matthew was killed with a sword somewhere in Ethiopia. Mark died in Alexandria, after being dragged through the streets. Luke was hanged from an olive tree in Greece. John—the only disciple not to die as a martyr—endured boiling in oil and later was banished to Patmos. Peter was crucified upside down in Rome. James the Greater was beheaded in Jerusalem. James the Lesser was thrown from the pinnacle of the Temple, and when that didn't kill him he was beaten to death with a club. Bartholomew was flayed alive. Andrew was bound spread-eagle to a cross. Thomas was run through with a lance somewhere in India. Jude was riddled with arrows. Matthias, the man elected to replace Judas, was first stoned and then beheaded. Barnabas of the Gentiles was stoned to death. The great apostle Paul was beheaded in Rome after a long and grueling missionary career.

Doesn't sound much like contemporary Christianity in the Western world, does it? Faith isn't easy in the Kingdom of God. It takes deep roots—a persevering commitment to Christ above all else—for a person to be willing to endure ill treatment.

THORNY PROBLEMS

The story doesn't end there. Another type of hearer makes a good start but also falls short. Like the stony ground, this soil provides a good start for the seed, allowing it to sprout and grow. However, before long the plant is choked. With the rocky ground, shallow roots prevent the plant from being prepared for tribulation and persecution. Another pair of attackers chokes the life from this plant: "worry of the world and the deceitfulness of wealth" (Matthew 13:22).

Anxiety was no stranger to the people of Jesus' day and it is no stranger to us. Making a living consumes more than time, it consumes our thoughts and efforts. Add to that the false idea that wealth brings peace and happiness and what is left is an individual on the treadmill of life, working, struggling, worrying about work and wealth, with no place for faith.

The problem stems from how we perceive faith. What Jesus describes has been a problem from the very beginning. Many, perhaps most people, see faith as an additive to life, something to mix with everything else we experience. Jesus meant the gospel message to be much more. He intended it to be the whole, not the part. It is the core, the structure, the very life of a believer. When reduced to anything less, it becomes a mere element of life, not life itself.

This is the difference between religious thinking and Kingdom thinking. Religious thinkers see faith as a tool, a help, an additive to life. Kingdom thinkers see faith as the beginning, middle, and end of life. They cannot see themselves apart from faith. Their thoughts, goals, and desires are all bathed in the light of spiritual belief. Religious thinkers see their spiritual service as part of what makes them whole, like one room in a large house, while Kingdom thinkers see faith as the house itself. Everything fits into faith; faith is too large to fit into anything else.

Jack Cavanaugh wrote the *American Family Portrait* series, books that follow the lives of a family through many generations and show the effects a family Bible has on them. In the second book, *The Puritans,* a father seats himself at the dinner table and asks, "Well, now, what can we do for God this day?"[3] Twenty-first-century religious thinkers ask, "What can God do for me?"

Religious thinkers often see belief as something that helps them. True as that is, it isn't the purpose of the Kingdom. Rather than making us wealthy and carefree in this life, the Kingdom, under the headship of Christ, exists to bring eternal glory to God and everlasting joy and fulfillment to His followers.

It is important to take care of day-to-day matters, to succeed in our businesses, to help our children through school, to plan for our future, but it is easy to slide down the slippery slopes of the pursuit of wealth and avoidance of worry. Such priorities choke the life out of promising people.

GROWING WHERE YOU'RE PLANTED

The success portion of the story comes last and is deceptively simple. "And the one on whom seed was sown on the good soil, this is the man who hears the word and understands it; who indeed bears fruit and brings forth, some a hundredfold, some sixty, and some thirty."[4] In other words, hearing + understanding = fruit.

Apart from the abundant yield of the good soil, there is sadness in this parable. The gospel message goes out freely, but only a portion—in the parable it's just one in four hearers—takes it for what it is. Jesus is not teaching that exactly 25 percent of hearers will be fruitful and 75 percent will fail, but He is teaching that the majority of those who hear the gospel will do nothing with it.

In each of the failings, the farmer sows the word, but the hearers fail to incorporate the truth. They may receive the word and express joy over it, but never make it an integral part of their lives. Here, the seed falls on good soil that nobody can remove, allows for root growth, and is free of choking weeds. The result is a harvest thirty, sixty, or even as much as one hundred times greater than itself. Such production would amaze a farmer then and now.

What makes the difference? Each heard, but only one "understood." In Jesus' teaching, understanding means putting truth side by side with life, joining them into a single, vital unit. That is the key to success in the Kingdom of God, and that understanding is what was missing in those represented by the soil that produced no fruit.

No wonder Jesus says, "So take care how you listen; for whoever has, to him more shall be given; and whoever does not have, even what he thinks he has shall be taken away from him" (Luke 8:18). Fruitful living is not possible until we allow the seed of God's Word to penetrate our hearts.

FOR REFLECTION

1. In this parable, what does the seed represent? the soil?
2. What does this parable teach us about the reasons not everyone believes when they hear the gospel?
3. Consider the four types of soil and what they represent. How would you explain their meanings?
4. In what ways would you like to be more "Kingdom productive" in your family, church, work, etc.?

CHAPTER 7

That Tares It

The devil is a better theologian than any of us and is a devil still.   A. W. TOZER

Jesus presented another parable to them, saying, "The kingdom of heaven may be compared to a man who sowed good seed in his field.

"But while his men were sleeping, his enemy came and sowed tares among the wheat, and went away.

"But when the wheat sprouted and bore grain, then the tares became evident also.

"The slaves of the landowner came and said to him, 'Sir, did

you not sow good seed in your field? How then does it have tares?'

"And he said to them, 'An enemy has done this!' The slaves said to him, 'Do you want us, then, to go and gather them up?'

"But he said, 'No; for while you are gathering up the tares, you may uproot the wheat with them.

"'Allow both to grow together until the harvest; and in the time of the harvest I will say to the reapers, "First gather up the tares and bind them in bundles to burn them up; but gather the wheat into my barn. . . ."'"

Then He left the crowds and went into the house. And His disciples came to Him and said, "Explain to us the parable of the tares of the field."

And He said, "The one who sows the good seed is the Son of Man, and the field is the world; and as for the good seed, these are the sons of the kingdom; and the tares are the sons of the evil one; and the enemy who sowed them is the devil, and the harvest is the end of the age; and the reapers are angels.

"So just as the tares are gathered up and burned with fire, so shall it be at the end of the age.

"The Son of Man will send forth His angels, and they will gather out of His kingdom all stumbling blocks, and those who commit lawlessness, and will throw them into the furnace of fire; in that place there will be weeping and gnashing of teeth.

"Then 'The righteous will shine forth as the sun' in the kingdom of their Father. He who has ears, let him hear."

MATTHEW 13:24-30, 36-43

F RANK Abagnale is a world-renowned expert on forgery and document security. He has lectured FBI agents for over two decades. That's what he's known for now. He used to be a fraud. As a young man, he pretended to be a number of things he was not, including an airline pilot and medical doctor. From the time he was sixteen until he was twenty-one, he forged bad checks and ran from the law. He served prison time in France, Sweden, and the United States. The Steven Spielberg movie *Catch Me If You Can* is based on his life and his book by the same name. Now a respected businessman, Abagnale has become a living testimony that not everything is what it appears. Deception can come cloaked in the guise of respectability.[1]

Jesus wanted to make this same point about the Kingdom of God. To do so, He turned again to the practices, implements, and even the stock crop of agriculture. His crowd knew all about wheat, the focus of this second parable on the Kingdom. Few sights are as beautiful as a mature wheat field with its undulating waves made to pulse by the wind. It seems alive.

Wheat and other grain produce were not only beautiful in the fields, they were critical to life in the first century. Bread was a dietary staple. When there was an abundance of wheat, there was joy; when there was a drought the wheat died and people wallowed in debilitating hunger. Many things could destroy a crop: drought, too much rain, and sabotage. That's right, sabotage. People had enemies then as people have them now. Agricultural wars are not limited to our time.

When Jesus tells this parable about the Kingdom of Heaven, He has the attention of everyone present. It is a story of hard work, of business, and of intrigue. Like a novel, it has a protagonist who must fend off an evil antagonist who is set to ruin him. The real message behind the parable is that in the world, not everything is what it seems. Mimics, imposters, and counterfeits populate the world in general and the Christian world specifically.

Why does God allow it? Why doesn't God remove all the evil people? There is a reason and in that reason is revealed another mystery about the Kingdom of Heaven.

SORT OF SIMILAR BUT VERY DIFFERENT

After reading this parable, we might be tempted to say that it is very similar to the parable of the soils. Both have to do with plants, farming, and harvesting. In less holy moments, we might think that Jesus just put a new twist on an older tale. That is incorrect. The two parables are far more different than they are alike, and in those differences new facets of the Kingdom are revealed.

Unlike the parable of the soils, the seed in this story is not the Word of God but the *people* of God. As in the first parable, a man goes out into the field and broadcasts seed in every direction. In this case, the seeds are believers who grow where planted; the field is the world, not the heart of the person.

Jesus later explains to the disciples that He is the sower. It is He who plants believers throughout the world. They grow, pushing out the boundaries of the Kingdom. Unlike the first parable, which features only one sower, a second sower appears in this one. This imposter brings a different kind of seed that he, under the protective darkness of night, secretly plants in the same field. This treacherous act has only one purpose: to destroy the hard work of the farmer. It is a mission to destroy.

A QUICK LESSON IN WEEDS

To comprehend the parable, we need to understand exactly what is taking place. Jesus tells of a second sower who spreads "tares" in the field. A tare is a weed, but not just any weed. As a seed and young plant, a tare looks very much like wheat. Most likely, the plant Jesus has in mind is the bearded darnel, a type of rye grass. Darnel produces a black head and can be poisonous. What makes this act so diabolical is that the weeds grow with the wheat and no one is the wiser until weeks or months later when they begin to produce the grain head.

Like the workers in the story, we might be tempted to run out and weed the field, but that would be far more destructive than letting the seed grow. By the time the darnel is distinguishable from the wheat, it has had a chance to let its root system grow—one that is intertwined with the roots of the good plants. To remove the one was to uproot the other. The cure was worse than the disease.

The farmer makes the difficult but correct decision when he says, "Allow both to grow until the harvest." Any other decision would end in the total loss of the crop, exactly the imposter's plan.

THE ORIGINAL PLAN

The parable of the tares mixes the beautiful image of God's success with the ugly fact that evil exists and works against His plan. In the story, Jesus describes the hardworking farmer, his servants, and the field that they plant. Their goal is noble and they do everything right. But someone is dedicated to their failure.

In the previous parable of the soils, Jesus says that some seed falls on hard, foot-trampled ground and that the evil one comes and snatches it away. In other words, the devil works to keep the gospel from settling in the heart of the hearer. His work does not end there, however. What can Satan do about those who do understand and accept the gospel? This parable doesn't show Satan trampling the seedlings or burning them as they mature. He is unable to uproot them himself, so he takes another strategy. If he can't conquer, then he will contaminate.

It's comforting to know that Satan has no control over our spiritual standing or growth. He cannot keep the seed from sprouting and maturing. Unlike God, he is not all-powerful. One of the persistent myths among Christians is that Satan is the opposite of God. He's not. Unlike the Creator, Satan is limited in many ways. He is not omniscient, omnipotent, or transcendent. He is certainly craftier, smarter, more experienced, and more powerful than humans are, but God has placed limitations on what and how he can affect the believer. It is a mistake to underestimate the devil, but it is equally a mistake to live in fear of him.

Although Satan can't uproot us, he can do his share of damage. He cannot remove the truth from the believers' minds, but he can introduce counterfeits. A literal translation reveals that the devil "sowed upon" that wheat field. This oversowing mixes the bad with the good. It's a devious idea meant to discourage believers and destroy the credibility of the gospel. The result is the Kingdom of Heaven becomes a mixed bag of believers and fake followers.

THE ORIGINAL SCHEME

No matter how many times I read the New Testament, I am amazed at how much of it addresses false teaching. At least eleven New Testament books contain comments about false teachers such as Judaizers, Gnostics, and other unnamed troublemakers. If we include the four Gospels with their many mentions of Pharisees, Sadducees, and scribes and the book of Acts with its account of Judaizers, the number climbs to sixteen–sixteen out of twenty-seven books explicitly warn about false teachers.

The New Testament shows that the early church was plagued with problems from within and without. Persecution from without was painful, frightening, and intimidating, but the gospel went forward nonetheless. Most historians believe that the persecution was like water on an oil fire, spreading instead of extinguishing the truth. A more pervasive problem came from within the ranks. Almost every epistle in the New Testament deals with internal church problems. Peter writes, "But false prophets also arose among the people, just as there will also be false teachers among you, who will secretly introduce destructive heresies, even denying the Master who bought them, bringing swift destruction upon themselves" (2 Peter 2:1).

Secretly introduce destructive heresies? Sound familiar? What Jesus foretells in this parable comes soon after the birth of the church. Paul spends three chapters warning the Corinthians about those who preach a different gospel and seek glory for themselves: "These people are false apostles. They are deceitful workers who disguise themselves as apostles of Christ. But I am not surprised! Even Satan disguises himself as an angel of light" (2 Corinthians 11:13-14, NLT).

The problem continued long enough and was serious enough to cause John to write a warning to the church: "Beloved, do not believe every spirit, but test the spirits to see whether they are from God, because many false prophets have gone out into the world. By this you know the Spirit of God: every spirit that confesses that Jesus Christ has come in the flesh is from God; and every spirit that does not confess Jesus is not from God; this is the spirit of the antichrist, of which you have heard that it is coming, and now it is already in the world" (1 John 4:1-3). John was warning us to watch for the tares among the wheat.

Even the little New Testament book of Jude raises an alarm. So severe was the internal disruption from the "tares" that Jude was compelled to change the topic of his letter: "Beloved, while I was making every effort to write you about our common salvation, I felt the necessity to write to you appealing that you contend earnestly for the faith which was once for all handed down to the saints. For certain persons have crept in unnoticed, those who were long beforehand marked out for this condemnation, ungodly persons who turn the grace of our God into licentiousness and deny our only Master and Lord, Jesus Christ" (Jude 1:3-4). His words ring with familiarity. "For certain persons have crept in unnoticed. . . ." sounds very much like Jesus' words, "But while his men were sleeping, his enemy came and sowed tares among the wheat, and went away."

The apostle Paul asks one church, "You foolish Galatians, who has bewitched you?" (Galatians 3:1). The problems that afflicted the early church are the same as those that trouble us today. God's wheat field continues to thrive, but it comes with its share of weeds.

ARTIFICIAL PLANTS AND PLASTIC FRUIT

In 1994, a court convicted Aldrich Ames of espionage. Ames had been a trusted employee of the CIA for thirty-two years. He was the highest-ranking CIA officer ever charged with criminal activity. He compromised ten Eastern European double agents, all of whom were killed. He also laid bare the identities of over twenty U.S. intelligence officers and other CIA operatives. Before his arrest, he appeared the model employee, loyal and patriotic. Only a handful had suspicions. To see him was not to see treachery, just a family man serving his country in the intelligence business. But for a payoff of two million dollars from Moscow connections, Ames was willing to release information that proved deadly. His outward appearance and speech concealed his real nature. Just as the CIA has its share of counterfeits, so does the church. It is unavoidable, and shocking as it is, we should expect it.

Over the years, I have heard countless times, "The church is filled with hypocrites." Critics are fond of saying it as if that reality is the death knell of the church. They're shocked when I agree with them and are even more astonished when I tell them that Jesus said it would be that way from the beginning.

WHY GOD ALLOWS EVIL IN YOUR NEIGHBORHOOD

There is no spiritual herbicide we can apply to the weeds in the church. The hard truth is that nothing can be done about them—nor should be. The last part may sound strange. We often think that the world—or at least the church—should be a perfect place. We think evil should be locked outside our sanctuary doors and only the pure of heart should be able to cross its threshold, sit in its pews, and sing its songs. Perhaps in a better world such would be the case, but our world is what it is. It is the world in which we serve God.

Why does God allow it? Why not put scythe to weed and be done with it? That day will come. Jesus portrayed it as the harvesttime when the angels will gather the good and the evil will be bundled and burned. The farmers in earshot of Jesus understood the image. It was what one did with weeds, discarded branches, and other useless product. In a day when wood was hard to gather, having anything to burn was a luxury, even if it was just weeds.

We must face another fact: We, the servants, are ill equipped to tell the difference between the tares and the wheat. Like the workers in the parable who desired to run out and begin yanking weeds, we must wait for the right time. Someone we might assume to be a "weed" may be in the process of becoming a person of faith. In our eyes, he may seem an imposter, but an encounter with Christ a day, week, or decade later may change that. It is difficult to distinguish between someone in the process of becoming a Christ follower and someone who is a perpetual pretender. Such things should be left to God who can read the heart.

BEING GENUINE AND DETECTING COUNTERFEITERS

The mystery revealed in this Kingdom parable is simple to understand but sometimes hard to swallow. We have a strong sense of perfection, a sense of what ought to be. We're dissatisfied when we learn that purity is out of reach. There will be a time for the ideal, a time when perfection becomes the norm and threats from without and corrosion from within will be mere history. Only God knows when that will be. Until then, we are to grow where we are, to hear, practice, and teach the truth. We are also to pray for those around us.

In Greece, high atop a rock prominence, sits the Monastery

of the Holy Trinity. It is a type of monastery called *meteora.* The word comes from the Greek *meteoron* that means "something raised up," or "to hover in air." The hallmark of this structure and others like it is its elevation and seclusion. Built around 1475, the cross-in-a-square building sits on a high rock outcropping that looks like an extended, arthritic thumb. The purpose of such retreats was to provide a place away from a world of wickedness. Building materials, supplies, food, and even people were hauled up hundreds of feet by rope. Despite the best efforts of the monks and builders, "tares" found their way in, including squatters and, during World War II, German and Italian soldiers who looted the structure.

In over two decades of ministry, I have worked in the church with men and women who are actively teaching, serving, and administrating, only to discover that they have been involved in some chronic sin and feel no remorse for it. On several occasions, I have sat opposite a man who was cheating on his wife, avoiding his children, hurting his friends. I wondered how an adult Sunday school teacher or other church leader could arrive at such a place.

"You don't understand," one man told me. Unfortunately I did. He left my office, left the church, left his family, and left me with questions. John writes, "They went out from us, but they were not really of us; for if they had been of us, they would have remained with us; but they went out, so that it would be shown that they all are not of us" (1 John 2:19). Tares among wheat.

We can't deny that evil exists. There's no escaping it. How stunning it is to realize that the first two Kingdom parables feature the presence and activity of Satan. The church was not founded in isolation nor meant to be inaccessible on a hilltop. Instead it's been placed where it can do the most good, mixed into the world that needs it so much. That means that wheat grows next to tares, but at least the wheat grows.

During World War II, C. S. Lewis delivered a number of informal radio addresses that were later compiled into best-selling books. His broadcasts were designed to restore hope to battle-weary Britons. One of his comments sounds as if it could just as easily have been written to remind battle-weary Christians why God is so patient: "*Now* is our chance to choose the right side," he said. "God is holding back to give us that chance. It won't last forever."[2] Jesus accepts that the Kingdom is tainted from without by those who sit within, but His love for the wheat is greater than His anger over the tares.

FOR REFLECTION

1. Identify the "players" in the parable of the wheat and tares.
2. Why was planting tares among wheat such a devious act?
3. Why didn't the farmer have the tares pulled as soon as he learned of his enemy's sabotage?
4. What does this parable show us about the limits of Satan's power over believers?
5. How prevalent do you believe false teaching is in the church today? How can you guard yourself–and others within your family or church–against it?

CHAPTER 8

A Little Mustard Is a Good Thing

The church is an organism that grows best in an alien society.
C. STACEY WOODS

He presented another parable to them, saying, "The kingdom of heaven is like a mustard seed, which a man took and sowed in his field; and this is smaller than all other seeds, but when it is full grown, it is larger than the garden plants and becomes a tree, so that 'the birds of the air' come and 'nest in its branches.' "
MATTHEW 13:31-32

DOLLARS seem to flow continuously through the doors of Apple Computer and Microsoft Corporation. In 2003 alone Apple raked in more than $6 billion; Microsoft, an astonishing $32 billion. Today these companies wield enormous influence, but in the early 1970s it would have required great imagination to watch Steven Jobs and Stephen Wozniak assembling computers in Jobs' garage and predict how these two men would change the world, as would their competitors Bill Gates (now the wealthiest man in the world) and Paul Allen, founders of Microsoft. It is unlikely that even these farsighted entrepreneurs could have envisioned their impact.

As mind-boggling as their success is, it is nothing compared to what God does through the insignificant. Every tour I make through the Bible reminds me that the pattern of God's work is to invest His power in the weak and empower the unexpected. I've concluded that God specializes in the small, the tiny, the minimal, turning them into unimagined successes, giants that leave impressions wherever they stand. Out of a word came a cosmos; out of one couple was born humanity; out of one man was born a nation; a shepherd boy became a king; mud became an agent in healing; and a boy's lunch fed multitudes.

Out of the apparent insignificance of a wandering Jewish teacher came the most powerful force the world has seen. Theologians have written much about the coming of Christ as a baby. Each year, most of the world celebrates Christmas in one manner or another. In the twenty-first century, it is buried in crass commercialism, credit cards, gift giving, expensive toys, and more, but the truth of Christ's coming somehow still shines through. Each time we revisit it, the story becomes more amazing. Jesus came as a baby. Nothing human could be smaller; nothing could be more helpless than an infant. It is amazing to think that Jesus went through gestation: From zygote to fetus, from fetus to infant, from infant to child, and then into his teenage years.

"The angel answered and said to her, 'The Holy Spirit will come upon you, and the power of the Most High will over-shadow you; and for that reason the holy Child shall be called the Son of God'" (Luke 1:35). The words are simple but the concept is soul shaking. How the Holy Spirit came upon Mary is unknown. The biological mechanism is beyond the biblical text. Just like Creation in Genesis, the *how* is unimportant when compared to the fact of what is. Still, to ponder Jesus in the womb moves us to amazement. Jesus did not appear out of the clouds, did not come as conquering warrior-king wielding a sword to strike down sin and oppression. Although Jesus has always existed, the physical, earthly Jesus we know came microscopically, then as a child, who like all infants was dependent upon others for survival.

Since the arrival of my grandson, Josiah, a few months ago, I have thought of this. When I first held him, it occurred to me that his well-being was in the strength of my arms and the focused attention of my thoughts. Carelessness on my part could mean disaster for the little person I held. Someday he will run and jump and play ball, but for now he is depend-ent on those around him—a tiny package of humanity, a sample of what he may become—unable to sit up on his own. As an infant, Jesus was no different.

As an adult, Jesus was a carpenter from a little known and unimportant town who turned into an itinerate preacher with a ragtag following of fishermen, tax collectors, and outcasts. Surely observers would not have thought these men would ever amount to much or that their impact would last long. They were wrong. Two millennia later, the church founded by Christ has reached every corner of the globe with no indication that it will ever dissolve. If we could peer back in time to see the disciples in the upper room before Pentecost, we would be hard-pressed to see anything but a band of disheartened, frightened, cowered, and confused people wondering what to do next. Acts 2 describes how all that changed in a day.

OUT OF THE TINY GROWS THE MIGHTY

The growth of the church after Pentecost was startling, but Jesus provided a preview of its rapid development in this third Kingdom parable. After telling two long, detailed parables and then providing explanations for them, Jesus uses just forty-five words (in the original Greek) to tell the parable of the mustard seed. It is a microparable with a megameaning. Here is a picture of success in the face of mountainous odds.

One of the great mysteries of the Kingdom is its arrival in such an unexpected way. The people of Jesus' day "knew" how the Messiah, their Great Deliverer, would arrive—or at least they thought they did. Visions of a mighty steed mounted by a conquering Savior whose sword dripped with Roman blood filled their minds. Jesus arrived in the opposite way: humble parents, tiny town, out-of-the-way birth in an unexpected place, common laborer, and a message that didn't fit with centuries of hopes and desires. As we saw in the parable of the soils, only a minority heard and responded with understanding. For Jesus and the believers of the Kingdom it was an uphill march.

This parable is a story of comparison and expectation. Small and seemingly insignificant, the mustard seed sometimes grows as high as ten to fifteen feet in a single season.

Jesus makes a simple statement about the seed that people quibble over to this day: "And this is smaller than all other seeds." The epiphytic orchid seed is actually the tiniest seed of all. It takes 28 million seeds to make an ounce.[1] But note that Jesus does not say that the mustard seed is smallest in the world. Certainly He knows what those around Him do not, that other seeds exist that are much smaller. Does this mean that Jesus spoke a factual error? Of course not. The context of the parable deals with plantable seeds familiar to the listener.

There are three thousands species of mustard.[2] We have no idea which seed Jesus had in mind, nor does it matter. The seed itself is unimportant. What matters is the contrast.

We had help in the first two parables. Jesus tells His disciples the meaning of those stories, laying out the significance of each representative element. Two thousand years later, we get to listen in. This parable, however, comes with no explanation. We have to apply prayerful, thoughtful consideration. Of course, that's the purpose of a parable.

Comparing this parable with the two we've already seen, we immediately encounter some obvious differences. These differences are important. The question is, should this parable be considered an extension of the others? The answer is no. By looking at the differences, the teaching becomes clearer.

The obvious distinction is that Jesus mentions only one seed, not the many used in broadcast sowing or that would result in a field of wheat. Here a gardener plants a single seed and the result is a single plant. A field of mustard plants would be devastating to the rest of the garden. The farmer needs only one plant for his purpose. The result is growth beyond expectation.

This is a parable of stark contrasts. The important element compares the tiny with an unexpected result. Even twenty-first century minds have trouble understanding how something that measures fifteen feet high can come from something as tiny as a mustard seed. Nothing known to the people of Jesus' day was tinier or more symbolic of insignificance.

GROWING LIKE A WEED

Just like the mustard plant, the Kingdom and the church that represents it would grow with dramatic speed. Approximately fifty days after Jesus' crucifixion, on the day of Pentecost, the church was born, and it came in with a bang. The book of Acts tells that Peter and the other disciples, now empowered by the Holy Spirit, proclaimed a message that could not be ignored, a sermon that burrowed into the heart of the listeners. Peter—a man who weeks before was so intimidated by probing questions that he denied with a solemn oath ever knowing Jesus—stood in the midst of a large crowd and let loose a sermon that could make angels weep. When he finished, three thousand people responded in faith and baptism. The tiny church had become a megachurch in a single day. But it didn't end there. "And the Lord was adding to their number day by day those who were being saved" (Acts 2:47). Every day the numbers grew; daily the ranks of believers swelled to amazing numbers. So startling was this growth that it precipitated persecution.

After a dramatic healing, the numbers spiked again. "But many of those who had heard the message believed; and the number of the men came to be about five thousand" (Acts 4:4). That was just the men. We don't have hard and fast numbers, but counting women and children, the number could easily have topped ten thousand or more. All of this happened in a matter of days.

One day a small group of discouraged, beaten disciples was still puzzling over Christ's resurrection appearances and his ascension; days later thousands of people publicly claimed Jesus as Savior. Mustard-seed men became part of something far greater than anyone could imagine.

GUESTS IN THE BRANCHES

Another controversial element in this parable has nothing to do with the heart of the illustration, but with a single element mentioned by Jesus: "So that the birds of the air come and nest in its branches." Some see the birds as evil or as a reference to Satan and his minions. Although birds represent Satan in the parable of the soils, we should not assume it means the same here. Jesus mentions nothing evil in reference to these birds or any actions they take. They just arrive and perch on the branches—much as people find rest and refuge in God's Kingdom.

From time to time, someone says to me, "You'll never see my husband in church. He hates the church." I've also heard this said about wives, brothers, sisters, fathers, and mothers, and each time I do, I have to hold back a smile. Images flutter by my mind's eye like migrating butterflies—images of the people who said they'd never come to church. Some are deacons now, some ordained ministers, and others are financial pillars, witnesses, or teachers. These "birds" found their way to Christ and found branches upon which they could rest. Some arrived sooner and some came more easily than others, but there they were, faces I saw every Sunday. Their arrival was unexpected but nonetheless real. It surprised those who knew them—it even surprised the newcomers—but it didn't surprise Jesus. That's how the church is to operate. The branches spread and the birds come, and they find it far more accepting and comfortable than they had imagined.

Actually, the birds are not as significant to this parable as the branches upon which they sit. Remember, this is a parable of contrast, comparing the tiniest with the largest. By confining ourselves to the simple beauty of the parable, we see the majestic power of it: Not only does a mighty plant grow from a small seed, it grows to such a stature that birds can roost in its branches. Mark's account of this parable uses the phrase "large branches" (Mark 4:32).

WHAT WAS MEANT TO BE

It's a simple parable with profound meaning, one that reveals a secret now revealed. That mystery is the church. Jesus only founded one institution, and His love for that organization is beyond measure. Paul writes, "Christ also loved the church and gave Himself up for her" (Ephesians 5:25). Love like that is impossible to ignore.

The church is Christ's representative on earth, and each member serves as an ambassador for the Kingdom. The church is a beacon in the darkness of the world. Although its history has been rugged, marred, besmirched, and even bloodied, it remains the instrument of God's choice. And what an odd choice it seems.

If the church was viewed from a strictly business paradigm it would be considered a phenomenal success. No organization so covers the world and welcomes people of every color, background, and education. No institution has endured so long, suffered so many attacks, yet continued to thrive and exert an influence that alters the heart and mind of humankind. In the two thousand years since the Day of Pentecost recorded in Acts 2, nations have flowered and then wilted into the history books; thrones of royalty have eroded and been replaced by other forms of government; movements have arisen only to disappear. The church, however, remains, rooted in the soil of every continent, growing in freedom and oppression alike.

There are organizations that look like churches, talk like churches, meet like churches but have very little to do with representing the Kingdom. That is to be expected. It has always been and will continue to be so until Jesus comes for the church He founded. A visible Kingdom church may have a denominational tag stitched to its garments but it goes beyond simple affiliation. The designation Baptist, Methodist, Presbyterian, or Lutheran does not make a church. Jesus makes a church. Where the church remains faithful to Christ, her groom; where God remains the object of worship; where ambassadors of the Kingdom gather–there is the church.

A FLY IN THE MUSTARD:
EXCHANGING SPIRITUALITY FOR ORGANIZATION

The great British Christian thinker and writer C. S. Lewis wrote a book called *The Screwtape Letters*. This is another work that began as a series of radio broadcasts during the dark days of World War II. In the book, Lewis describes the letters between young demon apprentice Wormwood and his "wise" uncle Screwtape. Screwtape comments: "One of our great allies at present is the Church itself. Do not misunderstand me. I do not mean the Church as we see her spread out through all time and space rooted in eternity, terrible as an army with banners. That, I confess, is a spectacle which makes our boldest tempters uneasy. But fortunately it is quite invisible to these humans."[3]

Lewis distinguishes between the church that most see and the church that Christ instituted. The valid church comes in a variety of colors, meets at different times, has different customs but always has Christ at its heart and God in its sights. We are often sloppy in our language. We drive down the street, see a brick building with a tall white steeple and say, "Look at that pretty church." There's no crime in that, but it is inaccurate. What we are seeing is the church building. The church is not built with hammer, nails, studs, and plywood. The church is made of flesh and blood and bone. If all church buildings suddenly disappeared, the church would remain.

A prime example is China, where the church, though largely unseen, flourishes in hundreds of house churches. For decades, the Chinese government has been trying to bring Christian churches under its control. Lawful religious activity is restricted to government-authorized organizations, such as the Three-Self Patriotic Movement, and all places of worship are to be registered. Yet despite intense persecution of Christians who refuse to submit to these regulations, the number of Christians in China has exploded—from 700,000 in 1949 to at least 35 million today.[4]

Like the mustard seed, the Kingdom started incredibly small only to spread its branches impossibly wide to cover the globe. It's exciting to know that the plant continues to grow and that we have a part in that expansion.

We stand on the informed side of the mystery of the Kingdom. For many of us this idea of the expanding church is not new and a little obvious. That's unfortunate. It is a wonderful revelation to see the vital, living, growing, expanding church for what it is, a miracle of divine design, powered by the sacrificial love of Christ. To be part of this body is humbling and thrilling.

GOD LOVES THE LITTLE

Jesus arrived in a small package, a mustard-seed Messiah, and the world has never been the same. Three decades later, He began a short ministry. Yes, even Jesus' ministry was small: just three years and twelve primary disciples, one of whom became a traitor. A larger group of over one hundred also numbered themselves with Jesus, but even that is a tiny group. Some churches have larger choirs.

From the outside, Jesus' ministry seemed a colossal failure: a handful of followers, most of whom abandoned Him during His trials and crucifixion. But that changed on that Pentecost day. A mustard-seed arrival, a mustard-seed ministry, all led to a gigantic Kingdom. The church became what Christ meant it to be and the rest is history—and the future.

In a borrowed tomb, they laid the dead Mustard Seed, and it gave birth to the Resurrection, the Ascension, and the church that would "upset the world" (Acts 17:6). God loves the small.

We struggle for significance in a world of more than six billion people. We want to count for something, to make some kind of difference, to have others notice us for some skill, art, contribution, or success, but we feel small in a world of giants. God loves the small, not because they are small, but because of what He can do with the discards of this world. Jesus is the prime example. Insignificant Jewish maiden, insignificant town, insignificant place of birth, insignificant nation, would seem to doom His life to a footnote in history. But God had other plans.

The church continues its work, its branches reaching further every year, and people from the most remote parts of the world find a place to roost. From the heart of the city to the edge of a rural town, Christ's church leaves its mark. From industrial nations to Third World countries, the church of Christ leaves an impression. No matter how tiny our ministry, no matter how insignificant our lives seem, we draw courage from the knowledge that God loves the small.

We are mustard-seed people who serve a mustard-seed Messiah born in a mustard-seed town. This Messiah later gathered mustard-seed disciples who watched their Savior die a mustard-seed death. But look at what the mustard seed yielded.

FOR REFLECTION
1. What does the mustard seed represent?
2. What does this parable teach you about the potential of your faith, no matter how weak it appears to be right now?
3. How does the growth of the church throughout the ages and around the world correspond to the lesson of this parable?
4. In what ways could Jesus be described as a mustard-seed Messiah?

CHAPTER 9

The Yeast We Can Do

Christians are trustees of a revelation who go out into the world calling men to accept and follow it. WILLIAM TEMPLE

[Jesus] spoke another parable to them, "The kingdom of heaven is like leaven, which a woman took and hid in three pecks of flour until it was all leavened." MATTHEW 13:33

NOTHING beats the smell of freshly baked bread. Its aroma is impossible to ignore. For centuries, people have been eating bread as a staple of their diet. In one form or another, almost every person on the planet has eaten bread. Today, we scoot down to the store or neighborhood bakery to pick up a fresh loaf. Getting bread is much easier than making it. Bread-making machines have replaced hard work and a strong pair of wrists. Still, many know, either from experience or from memories of watching Mom, the process of leaning over a lump of dough, kneading it, folding it, beating it, and then setting it in a pan to rise.

All of those within the hearing of this simple parable knew the image Jesus described. Making bread was a daily activity. A woman working the dough was a common sight and becomes, in the hands of Jesus, another revelation about the mystery of the Kingdom.

A BAKER'S THEOLOGY

The parable of the mustard seed is short but the parable of the yeast is even more abbreviated, just twenty-three words in the original language. The small size of the parable, however, does not dilute the power of it. This simple image unveils an important truth about the Kingdom, one that seems very similar to the one we've just examined, but that is different in an important way.

As with the parable of the mustard seed, this is a story of contrast and erroneous expectations. "The kingdom of heaven is like leaven, which a woman took and hid in three pecks of flour until it was all leavened." Is this a story about bread or about leaven? In all Bible study, the key is to look for the obvious before searching for the hidden. Here Christ compares the Kingdom to leaven.

Leaven, or yeast as we're used to calling it, is essential in bread-making. Yeast (*Saccharomyces cerevisiae*) is a fungus and reproduces in warm, carbohydrate-rich environments. As the microscopic organism multiplies, it produces carbon dioxide that is trapped in the dough and causes the bread to rise. Under a microscope, the yeast looks like a cluster of bubbles.

All of this may be common knowledge now, but it was an unknown process in the first century. No one had seen yeast. It wouldn't be until the seventeenth century when the likes of Robert Hooke and Antony van Leeuwenhoek would make strides in microscopic studies that anyone got a look at yeast. In Jesus' day, women saved a portion of dough from one batch to the next. How it worked, no one knew. It just worked. While a daily task, it must have been a puzzling thing to watch.

The word *leaven* (yeast) appears over twenty times in the Bible. The related Greek verb means "to ferment" or "to boil." It is a word of expansive influence. Once yeast is in the dough, there is no stopping it. Today we could hinder the process by freezing the dough, but first-century bakers knew that once they began the process there was no going back. So effective was yeast in infiltrating dough that it became an illustration of evil. In most cases in which the Bible mentions leaven, it represents sin.

Unleavened bread was part of Jewish culture and carried a significant spiritual image. During Passover, the bread was to remain unleavened. Since yeast was so pervasive, the baker made that bread away from all other dough to avoid accidental contamination.

Paul used this idea when he wrote to the Corinthians, "Your boasting is not good. Do you not know that a little leaven leavens the whole lump of dough? Clean out the old leaven so that you may be a new lump, just as you are in fact unleavened. For Christ our Passover also has been sacrificed. Therefore let us celebrate the feast, not with old leaven, nor with the leaven of malice and wickedness, but with the unleavened bread of sincerity and truth" (1 Corinthians 5:6-8).

Verses like these divide scholars. Is leaven always a sign of something evil?

TWO VIEWS OF LEAVEN

Open two Bible commentaries and chances are good that you will find two very different views about this parable. Some see the mention of leaven as a portrait of evil permeating the church, while others see the opposite. Those who think the yeast represents the contamination of the church cite passages that portray leaven in a negative way. One such passage is Matthew 16:6: "And Jesus said to them, 'Watch out and beware of the leaven of the Pharisees and Sadducees.'" Jesus' words certainly put the word in a negative light, as do other verses (Exodus 12:15; Leviticus 2:11; 6:17; 10:12; Luke 12:1; Galatians 5:8-9). Based on these passages, some scholars interpret this parable to mean that a little leaven will infect the church and continue to grow until it contaminates the whole body.

It's easy to understand why so many lean in that direction, but I think they are misguided. Context always dictates interpretation, which is why I also think it is incorrect to see the birds in the parable of the mustard seed as agents of evil in the midst of the holy. To assume that the leaven here represents evil because leaven does so elsewhere tortures the text. Peter writes to the church, "Be of sober spirit, be on the alert. Your adversary, the devil, prowls around like a roaring lion, seeking someone to devour" (1 Peter 5:8). Yet John in the book of Revelation describes Jesus as "the Lion that is from the tribe of Judah" (Revelation 5:5). The use of *lion* by Peter as a description of Satan's activities has no bearing on how we see the term used in reference to Jesus–same word, different context, different subject, and different application.

Not every use of the term *leaven* is negative. In fact, the Old Testament peace offering and thank offering required the giving of cakes of leavened bread.[1]

So what does the leaven in this parable represent? The leaven symbolizes the pervasive, growing power of the Kingdom, which like yeast, once started, cannot be stopped. The lump of dough is the world; the yeast is the message of Christ that moves through the world and through time. But isn't that the same as the parable of the mustard seed? Similar, yes, but not the same. The mustard tree grew from something insignificantly small to something noticeably large and attractive to passing birds. That parable describes the Kingdom from an *external* point of view. This story shows how the Kingdom works *internally*.

THE SPREAD OF GOOD

The gospel would go out; Jesus stated that on several occasions. Before His ascension, He commissioned the disciples to take the word beyond the borders of Jerusalem to the "remotest part of the earth."[2] But that is only part of the process. Taking the gospel out is mandatory; taking the gospel *in* is where faith becomes real. An outward growth of the Kingdom is thrilling, but the gospel changes lives one by one. Yeast becomes a good example of how the word of Christ alters the individual. That change always happens internally.

Christianity is ironic. Every Sunday, believers gather in the local church and worship. They do so by singing, praying, sharing, and immersing themselves in the Word of God. We do worship corporately, but we also do it individually. There can be no corporate worship if the individual is not involved in a personal, one-on-one encounter with God. This is clearest during the Lord's Supper. While traditions vary from denomination to denomination, the basic elements remain the same. The pastor leads the congregation in receiving the elements of bread and wine/juice. An observer might see this as an entire congregation coming to the Lord's Table, which is partly correct.

Yet while fifty, a hundred, or several thousand might participate in the ordinance, it is really a private thing. It is, as Calvin Miller described, "a table set for two."[3] If the mustard plant is the visible church, the physical representation of the Kingdom, then the leaven is the invisible, unstoppable power of faith to change the world one life at a time. Faith has always been the interaction of two: believer and God. This is the most important pairing in the world, a coupling of the divine with the human.

Probably the best-known verse in the Bible is John 3:16. Every child in Sunday school learns it: "For God so loved the world, that He gave His only begotten Son, that whoever believes in Him shall not perish, but have eternal life." So often we read this passage with a global view. There is no error in doing so, but the remarkable thing is that Jesus centers on the individual. Yes, God's love is global but the focus in this passage is on the singular "whoever."

Christ's disciples were a product of their day and, like those around them, expected a very visible Savior who would return Israel to its former greatness and glory. They expected the Kingdom to happen quickly, appearing full grown from its inception. No wonder the Pharisees viewed Jesus as "a monstrous parody of a Messiah," as Malcolm Muggeridge writes.[4]

Expectations, particularly long-held ones, often hold us back. In 1956, the famous underwater explorer Jacques-Yves Cousteau set a world record by dropping an anchor from his research ship *Calypso* over the Romanche Trench of the mid-Atlantic. The anchor tethered the ship with a five-and-a-half-mile nylon cord, achieving the world record anchorage of 24,600 feet. The *Calypso*, a former mine-sweeper, was held in place by an anchor over four and a half miles away. Distance made no difference. The anchor and nylon cable checked the ship's forward progress. Like that anchor, expectations can hold us back, even if those expectations are tied to an anchor set long before we were born. Jesus came with a different agenda from what the Jews expected the Messiah to have. He wanted people to change from within. Outward behavior is a function of inward thinking.

As strange as it may have sounded to His audience, God has always been concerned with the heart. He spoke through the Old Testament prophet Ezekiel and said, "Moreover, I will give you a new heart and put a new spirit within you; and I will remove the heart of stone from your flesh and give you a heart of flesh" (Ezekiel 36:26). Yeast changes the dough it inhabits; Jesus changes the lives of those in whom He resides. "And as a small piece of leaven placed in dough silently works until it leavens the whole lump, so will the kingdom spread until it fills the earth."[5]

WHAT'S GROWING INSIDE YOU?

The woman in this parable mixes (literally, "hides") the yeast with three pecks of flour. A peck is about twelve U.S. quarts. This means that our baker is working with thirty-six dry quarts of flour. When the baking is over, she will have nearly fifty pounds of bread, enough to feed over one hundred people. The idea is clear: The gospel will reach a great many people with its penetrating power. Like yeast, it will grow in the environment it inhabits until it permeates everything.

What's the mystery? Where's the secret? The mystery revealed to Jesus' listeners is that God's plan was to change people from within, not from without; to touch the soul of the person, not force conformity. Outwardly, the Kingdom grows in the form of churches dotting the face of the globe; inwardly it works one heart at a time. That was unexpected in Jesus' day, and it is unexpected today. Six and a half billion people populate our planet. If we could line the world's people in single file, the line would stretch over three million miles, long enough for six round trips to the moon. It's hard to feel significant in the face of such numbers, but we are just that–significant. The God who knows when every sparrow falls knows us by name. Christ died for each of the present six billion souls and for the billions who came before.

How does the gospel reach this many people? By growing in each believer who then shares the truth he or she has found in Christ. Amish friendship bread is a popular and meaningful tradition. Sometimes called the chain letter of baking, friendship bread is more about sharing than about baking. Someone gives a gift of starter that contains yeast. The recipient adds milk, flour, and sugar, and lets it rise. The new batch of dough is then divided. Some is baked and the rest is shared with other friends who repeat the process. Soon scores of people are making bread that originated with the first batch of starter. The gospel works the same way.

An old high school math problem demonstrates how a little sharing can go a long way. If we begin with a checker-board with sixty-four squares and place two pennies on square one, then double the number of pennies on square two and keep doubling it for each successive square, the amount of money on the sixty-fourth square is astronomical: $18,446,700,000,000,000,000. This principle of compounding is how yeast works and it is how the gospel works. One tells two, two tell four, and so on. Of course, as we saw in the parable of the soils, not all will hear and respond, but even a partial response produces a staggering number.

Chemists speak of catalysts. By definition, a catalyst is a substance that brings about a reaction without itself under-going a change. The purpose of yeast is not to be changed, but to change its environment. When introduced to bread dough, leaven begins to work but does not change the substance of the bread. Instead, it makes the bread better. The gospel is a catalyst. Christ is our catalyst. No matter when or where the gospel is preached, it changes lives without changing itself.

Unlike yeast and dough, however, we have a choice in the matter. We can be moved by the mystery or shield ourselves from its influence. To respond to the gospel is to allow spiritual alteration. That is why the Bible speaks of believers as being "born again" (John 3:3), buried and resurrected

(Romans 6:4), and a "new creation" (Galatians 6:15; see also 2 Corinthians 5:17).

The power to change the world rests in the simple act of internalizing God's Word and then sharing the truth.

FOR REFLECTION

1. According to the authors, what are the two views of the definition of leaven?
2. How did this parable, which focuses on inward change, conflict with the Jews' expectations of the kind of change the Messiah would usher in?
3. Are any expectations preventing you from allowing your faith to flourish as it might otherwise? (For instance, some people feel they can't trust God because He has allowed a serious illness, family situation, or other crisis to disrupt their lives.)
4. How does the Holy Spirit change people from within? Specifically, how has He worked within you to make you more Christlike?

CHAPTER 10

Treasure Hunter

The man who has God as his treasure has all things in one.

A. W. TOZER

The kingdom of heaven is like a treasure hidden in the field, which a man found and hid again; and from joy over it he goes and sells all that he has and buys that field.

Again, the kingdom of heaven is like a merchant seeking fine pearls, and upon finding one pearl of great value, he went and sold all that he had and bought it. MATTHEW 13:44-46

ON July 6, 1998, Lithuanian president Valdas Adamkus revealed a startling find. Thirteen years prior, workers installing a new air-conditioning system in the Vilnius Cathedral stumbled upon a treasure concealed in the walls. Experts believe the nearly 270 gold and silver religious works of art, many encrusted with precious stones, had been hidden in the cavity of the wall for 330 years. In 1655, Russian troops were ready to storm the city of Vilnius. Gold goblets, religious artifacts, and jewelry were tucked away for safekeeping. It worked. For over three centuries the treasure trove awaited discovery, but even after it was found, it was "buried" again. The Soviet Union still dominated Lithuania in 1985, and fearing what the USSR would do, local officials kept the find secret for another decade. Today, the treasure is valued at over one hundred million dollars.

Who among us hasn't dreamed of stumbling upon a fortune? Treasure stories were as popular in Jesus' day as they are now, and He used the fondness for such tales to unveil a new mystery about the Kingdom. He did so by telling twin parables, similar in many details but with telling differences.

What is the Kingdom of Heaven like? According to Jesus,

"The kingdom of heaven is like a treasure hidden in the field, which a man found and hid again; and from joy over it he goes and sells all that he has and buys that field" (Matthew 13:44).

THAR' BE TREASURE OUT THERE

It's a simple image with little detail and no explanation. Consequently, we are tempted to read details into the parable. Problems arise if we press the points of a parable too far. The result can be error instead of understanding. For example, some see an ethical dilemma in this tale. Is it right to find a treasure in a field you don't own, keep it hidden, and then buy it for yourself? That's pressing the issue too far and it misses the point. The beauty of these allegories is in their simplicity. The key has always been to find the single truth Jesus was teaching and to avoid adding to the mix.

In an age without banks (at least as we understand them), without safety deposit boxes or steel safes to protect money and valuables, people often buried their valuables in a place known only to them. This usually involved putting coins in a clay jar and burying it. The problem was that the treasure could be lost if the person who buried it died or forgot the location. During the Civil War, Southern landowners often buried their valuables on plantation property to keep them out of Yankee hands. Legend has it that such a treasure was buried on the grounds of the Walnut Grove plantation in 1864 as General Sherman's army was marching through South Carolina. Two family members died and the location of the treasure died with them. Perhaps that is the image Jesus is portraying here—a treasure long buried and unknown to others.

In any case, a man discovers the treasure, but buries it again. He then sacrifices everything he has in order to purchase the field and the secret treasure in it. Here is where people turn the meaning of the parable around. Some say that the meaning of the parable is our need to sacrifice all that we have in order to gain the Kingdom, which is far more valuable than anything we may have or own. While that is true, it is not the meaning of this story for several reasons.

First, Jesus is not a *hidden* treasure. No one is better known. He is the subject of more books than any other person or topic. He is the focus of movies, documentaries, radio programs, magazine articles, and much more. We also need to ask, if one finds Christ, does he "bury" Him again for another time? No, it's not Christ but something else that is hidden.

Second, one doesn't *find* Christ; Jesus finds the person. In salvation, God is the initiator. A few Scriptures help us see this. Jesus says, "No one can come to Me unless the Father who sent Me draws him; and I will raise him up on the last day" (John 6:44). The apostle John teaches, "We love, because He first loved us" (1 John 4:19). Perhaps the clearest statement on the matter is Jesus' assertion, "For the Son of Man has come to save that which was lost" (Matthew 18:11).

The most telling argument is that no one can purchase his or her salvation. "For the wages of sin is death, but the free gift of God is eternal life in Christ Jesus our Lord" (Romans 6:23). Salvation—entrance into the Kingdom—is always described as a gift, never as payment for work, never as something earned or deserved, but as something achieved by Christ.

Who then is the treasure seeker? It is none other than Jesus who makes the find.

ETERNAL INVESTMENT

Hidden in the field is a treasure that ignites "joy" in the finder—so much so that he reburies the find and hurries home to liquidate all his assets to make this single purchase. This is something he does gladly. What a perfect picture of Christ. The Savior searches for something He knows to have great value. When He finds it, He pays everything to get it. In this case, we are the treasure and Jesus sacrifices everything to make us His own. The author of Hebrews may have had this parable in mind when he encourages us to keep "fixing our eyes on Jesus, the author and perfecter of faith, who for the joy set before Him endured the cross, despising the shame, and has sat down at the right hand of the throne of God" (Hebrews 12:2). What joy could bring a person to suffer as Christ did? What joy could make the Cross look like an acceptable solution? We are the joy. Just as a treasure seeker is willing to sacrifice what he has to gain the riches he desires, so Jesus left heaven behind to purchase something He felt was of ultimate value—you.

This concept is the very heart of faith. All belief hinges on the understanding that Jesus sacrificed Himself for our benefit. Paul writes, "Being found in appearance as a man, He humbled Himself by becoming obedient to the point of death, even death on a cross" (Philippians 2:8).

THE DIFFERENCE BETWEEN TRASH AND TREASURE

We are treasure! What an amazing thought. Unfortunately, this concept has been lost to the contemporary church, which too often portrays the believer as unworthy of God's love, a hardened sinner, or as the old hymn describes it, nothing more than a worm. It is true that no person can claim a life so pure of sin as to merit a free pass into fellowship with God. It is equally true that we need to understand our own sinfulness to understand God's grace, but we should never view ourselves or others as worthless. Jesus sets our self-esteem. He is the standard. He holds us in high regard. We should value ourselves in the same way.

We are treasure, sought after and purchased by Christ. We are not worms, we are not worthless, we are people of infinite value to God. Jesus' seeking is active, purposeful, redemptive, liberating, and driven by a love we can only imagine. God does not base His love on our righteousness or legalism; He centers it in relationship. True, "there is no one who does good"[1] but there is a world of people loved by God. You are one of them.

A VERY PRICEY PEARL

The twin of the parable of the treasure is the parable of the pearl. "Again, the kingdom of heaven is like a merchant seeking fine pearls, and upon finding one pearl of great value, he went and sold all that he had and bought it" (Matthew 13:45-46). At first glance, the two stories seem identical, but there are significant differences that shed light on the Kingdom.

In ancient times, people considered pearls as valuable gems. Divers searched for pearls in the Red Sea, Indian Ocean, and the Persian Gulf. Occasionally, a pearl of enormous value was found, being worth the equivalent of millions of dollars today. As with anything of value, businesses arose around the industry. Merchants, like our jewelers, made it their job to search for the best.

The image is a simple one. A merchant is doing what he always does, seeking and purchasing quality pearls. He is used to seeing pearls of various qualities but is astounded to find the finest pearl he has ever seen. It is a pearl of such great value that he sacrifices all he has, selling his business, home, and valuables for the sole purpose of securing that one pearl. We're not told what made the pearl so valuable. Was it the size? its luster? its coloration? We don't know, nor does it matter. The important part of this parable isn't the nature of the pearl but the nature of the merchant.

The merchant is on a mission. We can imagine him traveling a great distance, meeting with divers, talking shop, sharing a meal, and examining their product. Perhaps a "wholesaler" produces a small bag and pours out all the pearls he has. The merchant has seen pearls before but the sight of one stuns him—a pearl he must possess at all costs. And it does cost all he has.

This is a story of recognition, desire, and sacrifice. Like the story of found treasure, the discovered object takes on a value unseen by others but recognized by the finder. But there are clear differences. First, unlike a treasure of man-made coins in a clay pot, the pearl is a natural product. It is the result of an irritant, usually sand, that has invaded the shell of a mollusk such as an oyster. The mollusk responds by producing nacre, the substance that covers the inside of the shell ("mother of pearl"). Over time, layer after layer of nacre is added until a pearl is formed. This natural process is the result of God's creative act. It is what God made mollusks to do. So while men may make treasures of coins, only nature can make a true pearl.

The treasure was hidden twice, first by the original owner and then by the finder until he could arrange to purchase the field. The pearl, on the other hand, was never hidden. Even though it grows secretly, it was meant to be found and sold to a merchant. Another difference is that the treasure hunter bought the field to obtain the treasure, but the pearl merchant bought just the pearl.

How do these differences add up? Some see the treasure as representing Israel and the pearl symbolizing the church. Perhaps so, but the clearest, most unambiguous interpretation is found in the simplicity of the tales. *Jesus is a complex teacher of simple truth.* The answer lies in numbers. A treasure is a compilation of things—in this case coins held in a clay jar and buried in a field. A pearl is a single "gem" that cannot be divided or cut into facets, unlike gems of stone. A diamond is plain looking when first taken from the ground. It is rough and encased in worthless stone. In the hands of a skilled diamond-cutter, it *becomes* something of great beauty. A pearl needs no alteration. It is what it is. While it might benefit from a good buffing, its shape remains the same.

The simplest interpretation is to see the treasure as faithful people buried in a field of disbelief. As Jesus carried out His mission, many came to believe in Him and many more rejected Him out of hand. The field is Israel, the place where Jesus walked and talked. Later it would include the world. The treasure is the sum of faithful believers in that barren field. So the treasure is belief in the face of great disbelief. To obtain those believers, Jesus died to buy the field.

The pearl, however, is a unity, a single entity that forces us to think not just of the many believers but of the one. Jesus not only died for the world (of which some would come to faith) but He died for the individual: your name on His lips; your face in His mind as He hung on the cross.

THE VALUE OF THE INVALUABLE

"By this the love of God was manifested in us, that God has sent His only begotten Son into the world so that we might live through Him" (1 John 4:9). The apostle John wrote those words many years after Christ's death, resurrection, and ascension. They're interesting words. While spoken in the plural–"manifested in us," "we might live"–it all hinges on an individual decision. We often think of faith in the multiple of congregations, churches, men's groups, Sunday schools, and the like, but faith remains one believer committing to one Savior.

John also records: "Jesus answered and said to them, 'This is the work of God, that you believe in Him whom He has sent'" (John 6:29). We can imagine the response of the crowd to those words: "What about sacrifices? What about feast days? What about the Temple tax?" Then as now there is a tendency to create complexity when the beauty of simplicity will do. God's assigned task for us is to believe.

Believing that Christ gave up everything and asks for nothing but faith from us changes how we view God, others, even ourselves. You are part of a treasure. You are a pearl. See that, and you will see that many around you are part of that same treasure found and bought by Christ, and they are pearls of exquisite beauty. This is not a call to arrogance. Christian self-esteem is in balance, in learning to color between the lines of extreme pride and improper, denigrating humility. That is the lesson of this Kingdom mystery. Jesus came looking for treasure and died to obtain it. You are that treasure.

FOR REFLECTION

1. In the first parable, what does the treasure represent?
2. In the second parable, what does the pearl represent?
3. What do these parables say about our worth in the eyes of Christ?
4. What are some of the similarities and differences between these two parables?

"Net" Profits

*God examines both rich and poor, not according to their lands
and houses, but according to the riches of their hearts.*

AUGUSTINE OF HIPPO

*Again, the kingdom of heaven is like a dragnet cast into the
sea, and gathering fish of every kind; and when it was filled,
they drew it up on the beach; and they sat down and gathered
the good fish into containers, but the bad they threw away.*

*So it will be at the end of the age; the angels will come forth
and take out the wicked from among the righteous, and will
throw them into the furnace of fire; in that place there will be
weeping and gnashing of teeth.* MATTHEW 13:47-50

THIS final Kingdom parable stands like a bookend to the others. Where the parable of the soils relates how the Kingdom started and each successive story emphasizes what the Kingdom is like, the parable of the dragnet shows how it will end. Twice in His seven Kingdom parables, Jesus uses the phrase "end of the age"—here and in the parable of the tares. Both deal with the divine separation of the good from the bad, with an unpleasant ending for the bad.

Jesus always set His parables in a work or home environment that would be familiar to His audience. This final Kingdom parable is no exception. Instead of a farmer's field or a baker's table, this parable is set on the Sea of Galilee, a harp-shaped freshwater lake approximately seven miles wide, thirteen miles long, and as much as 150 feet deep. It was and is a vital part of the region. Much of Jesus' ministry occurred around and on that lake. Fishing boats bobbed on its blue surface while fisherman plied their daily trade. A major roadway, the *Via Maris* ("Way of the Sea") came near the western side of the lake, which made the fishing industry even more prosperous. Fish, salted for preservation, were sent throughout much of the Roman world. To talk of fishing was to talk the people's language.

Several of Jesus' disciples had been working the nets since childhood. Peter, Andrew, James, and John knew all about the fish that swam beneath the surface and the different ways fishermen worked. They could use hook and line to pull the catch into the boat. This was fine for small catches but inefficient for those making a living from the sea. Usually fishing was done using one of three types of nets.

The first was a cast net that was worked by a single fisherman standing on the shore or on a small boat. The circular net was cast onto the water and then drawn back to the boat by a line. This was used to capture fish near the surface.[1] The second type of net common in Jesus' day was used to work in deeper waters. It operated much like a bag. The net was sunk and then drawn up quickly, hopefully with something in it.

The third kind of net was a dragnet.[2] Fishermen needed multiple boats to use it. The net, which had floats on the top and weights on the bottom edge, hung between two boats. After making a catch, it was dragged to shore.

The job of the Jewish fisherman using a dragnet continued with the landing of the catch, which had to be sorted. The Sea of Galilee hosted about forty different types of fish, but only a portion were permissible to eat. Mosaic Law restricted the kinds of fish that people could lawfully consume. Fish with fins and scales—like the tilapia, also known as St. Peter's fish—were permissible, but nothing else was. Catfish, eels, and shellfish were considered "abhorrent" and detestable.

Using a dragnet did not allow the fishermen to select the kind of fish they would catch. The net was nondiscriminatory. It pulled in whatever it encountered. We can see the fishermen on shore, up to their ankles in fish, pulling out catfish and eels, throwing them away. These weren't thrown back into the sea, but cast away for good. It made no sense to return the unusable fish to the water to reproduce.

ALL THE FISH IN THE SEA

In this parable, the Sea of Galilee represents the Kingdom. The fishermen and dragnet portray the angels gathering everyone in the Kingdom at the end of the age. Just as the parable of the tares illustrates, there are those who are in the Kingdom but not part of it. The net gathers them all, good and bad. Note the phrase "when it was filled." The picture is of a giant net that catches every fish. While human fishermen never catch every fish in the sea, that idea is there in this parable. Every fish is gathered and then a sorting process takes place.

Jesus uses a very strong word to describe the unwanted fish. Most translations render the term *sapros* as "bad," but it is more powerful than that. The word means worthless, repugnant, rotten, putrefied, and unfit. In the book of Leviticus, God tells the children of Israel that they were to consider fish that did not have the required scales and fins as "detestable things" (Leviticus 11:9-12)–not just unwanted but also loathed.

The workers did the separating with deliberation. They "sat down" and began to pick through the catch. They not only pulled out those that did not belong but also chose those that do belong. *This separation, then, is as much an act of love as it is of judgment.* Later, Jesus will repeat the teaching using the image of sheep and goats (see Matthew 25:31ff).

THE HARSH FACTS

Jesus breaks precedent with this parable by explaining its meaning without anyone asking Him to do so. "So it will be at the end of the age; the angels will come forth and take out the wicked from among the righteous" (Matthew 13:49). This is an active, deliberate, reasoned step. It is hard for some people to think of God as being a Judge. At times, we emphasize His love and kindness over the equally important aspect of His role as final Judge. Yet, the Bible is clear about it. For God to be God, He must be love, but He also must be just. That justice results in a harsh sentence.

". . . And will throw them into the furnace of fire; in that place there will be weeping and gnashing of teeth," adds Jesus (v. 50). This carried a greater shock to the Jews of Jesus' day that it does to us (and it's shocking to us). The messianic expectation for the Kingdom was that the Messiah would come, throw off the yoke of Rome's dominance, and free the people to live the life they deserved. Jesus shows that God would parcel out the righteous from evil but not in the expected way. Taking the parables together, we see that Jesus didn't emphasize lineage but faith; not heritage but belief.

Those deemed wicked face the "furnace of fire." Here is one of those verses we prefer to read over quickly and then move on. We'd rather not dwell on the idea of hell. However, this verse is a stop sign in the Gospels reminding us that God is just as well as loving and that there will be an end to His patience.

Theologians call this kind of divine justice "retributive justice." God has more than one level of justice. There is corrective justice, an act of God meant to put people back on the right track. Think of the punishments sent by God on the occasionally rebellious children of Israel as they wandered in the wilderness. The goal was not to destroy but to admonish, to correct behavior. There is also legislative justice. The Law of Moses is the best example of this. Clear laws about what could and could not be done were given, along with warnings about the punishment that would follow disobedience. What Jesus is describing is beyond those. It has finality to it. Louis Berkhof notes, "While in a sinless world there would be no place for its exercise, it necessarily holds a very prominent place in a world full of sin."[3] If God is holy, He must also be just. Berkhof also says, "While man does not merit the reward which he receives, he does merit the punishment which is meted out to him."[4]

No believer takes joy in knowing that eternal punishment will come to some people. It's doubtful God takes any pleasure in it. The great English Baptist preacher Charles Spurgeon said that preachers should preach about hell with tears in their eyes. Jesus didn't shy away from the topic. It was part of the message of the Kingdom and part of the mystery revealed. Here He uses the phrase, "weeping and gnashing of teeth." It is not the first time He uses the phrase. In fact, those words appear seven times in the Bible, six of them in the Gospel of Matthew.

We can't blame anyone for *wanting* to avoid the subject of eternal punishment, but it is irresponsible to actually do so. Chuck Colson sums it up well: "The doctrine of hell is not just some dusty, theological holdover from the Middle Ages. It has significant social consequences. Without a conviction of ultimate justice, people's sense of moral obligation dissolves, and social bonds are broken."[5]

Jesus had to teach the eternal consequences of choosing to live for oneself, rather than for the Kingdom. Not to do so would have been negligent and unfair to humanity. The message of the Kingdom is one of divine outreach, of inclusiveness, and of opportunity, but it is also one of responsibility. Some wish to do away with the concept of hell. To do so would throw the teaching and work of Christ out of balance. If there is no hell, there is no spiritual rescue and no need for Christ to have gone to the Cross. Jesus suffered to keep those who believe from suffering.

GOOD NEWS FOR FISH IS GOOD NEWS FOR US

While Jesus makes clear that the detestable fish will be cast aside, He also says that the good fish will be kept. A day will come when God will perfect the Kingdom. He will remove the tares and the unacceptable fish. (This may be the only case in which "fish" will be glad to have been caught!) After this separation, those God declares righteous because of their belief in Christ will live without the presence of evil.

Until that time, however, the Kingdom is a mixed bag, filled with believers who do their best to live in obedience to God, as well as those who have no time for the things of God. It is true for the world we see outside our window and it is true for what we see inside the doors of the church.

Christ makes clear that the Kingdom of Heaven is not perfect. "Beware of assuming that all who are swept into the power of God's kingdom are the children of the kingdom," says pastor and author John Piper. "The power of the kingdom gathers many (Matthew 7:22) into its net that will be cast out in the end because they loved healing not holiness;

they loved power and not purity; they loved wonders and not the will of God."[6]

The Founder is perfect, but not the Kingdom that bears His name. It contains "tares" and "unclean, detestable fish." The sin that will lead to separation is the sin of rejection–whether it comes subtly through the preoccupation with worldly things at the expense of godly things or by ignoring the message of Christ. The results are the same.

But the present mixture of the good and evil is not poor planning on God's part. It is opportunity for those who are willing to hear and believe to do so, but the time to choose is limited. The freedom of choice ends with either death or the second coming of Christ.

Sin permeates every fiber of society, but the good news is, this will end at some point. A life is coming that is untainted by sin. That freedom is impossible to describe, but every believer will experience it. The net catches everyone, but it is a joy to be caught by Christ.

FOR REFLECTION

1. Compare Matthew 13:47-50, the parable of the dragnet, with Matthew 25:31-46. What do these two passages reveal about what will occur at the end of the age?
2. What are the similarities and differences between this parable and the parable of the wheat and the tares, which was discussed in chapter 7?
3. What are the consequences for the "cast-off fish" in this parable? How is it possible that some church members may not end up in heaven?
4. Why is it dangerous to disregard the Bible's teachings on hell?
5. What hope does this parable provide for true Christ-followers?

MYSTERIES REVEALED IN THE KINGDOM PARABLES

Parables	Emphasis	Backdrop	Symbol	Formerly Hidden Expectations	Mystery Revealed
Soils	Expect a partial response	Mixed field	Soils	Universal acceptance	Partial acceptance
Tares	Expect imposters	Good field	Field		
Mustard	Expect rapid and startling external growth	Garden	A single plant	Exclusive	Inclusive
Leaven (Yeast)	Expect life-changing, inward growth	Bread dough	A microscopic catalyst	Change from without	Change from within
Treasure	Expect to be loved along with other believers	Someone else's field	Buried treasure	Acceptance by God based on national citizenship	God seeks the few believers
Pearl	Expect to be loved for yourself	"Wholesaler"	Extraordinary pearl	The individual doesn't matter	The individual is all that matters
Dragnet	Expect a separation of the true from the false	Sea	A fishing net	Kingdom changes everyone	Kingdom changes only some

PART THREE

The Mystery of the Church Age

CHAPTER 12

The Mystery of the Gospel

The gospel is so simple that small children can understand it, and it is so profound that studies by the wisest theologians will never exhaust its riches. CHARLES HODGE

With all prayer and petition pray at all times in the Spirit, and with this in view, be on the alert with all perseverance and petition for all the saints, and pray on my behalf, that utterance may be given to me in the opening of my mouth, to make known with boldness the mystery of the gospel, for which I am an ambassador in chains; that in proclaiming it I may speak boldly, as I ought to speak. EPHESIANS 6:18-20

IN 1991 businessman Brian Adkins had a sweet inspiration while listening to a Focus on the Family broadcast on Halloween. Wouldn't it be great, he wondered, if Christians could pass out candy enclosed in a wrapper that included a Bible verse? "If we could wrap the Word around the candy, every piece we gave out would have the possibility of planting a seed in a person's life," he said. Several years later, Adkins found some partners in the candy business and Scripture Candy was launched. The company's logo is an open Bible and the words "Go unto all the world and preach the gospel."[1]

Few words are as associated with Christianity as the simple, two-syllable word *gospel*. There are gospel music groups, gospel messages, gospel tracts, and even–thanks to people like Brian Adkins–gospel candy. Pastors encourage us to share the gospel, preach the gospel, hold the gospel, study the gospel, and spread the gospel.

The word *gospel* comes from a compound Greek word *euangelion*. The first part of the word (*eu*) means "good," the second part (*angelion*) refers to a message or messenger (we get our word angel from *angelion*). Most translate the word as "good news." In Old English *gode-spel* meant "good speech."

Originally, the term referred to both the message and the messenger. In the ancient Greek culture, the bearer of good news arrived with a smile on his face, a palm leaf in his hand, and a laurel on his spear. He would convey the welcome news and then receive a reward for being the lucky one to deliver it.[2] It was the opposite of "killing the bearer of bad tidings." In that sense, the news was good for both recipient and messenger.

The message of Christ fits this description better than any other message could. What better news could there be than of the Savior who came to release us from sin and His promise that eternal life awaits the person of faith? Used over seventy times in the New Testament, the word encapsulates the entire message of Christ. Mark starts his account with the words, "The beginning of the gospel of Jesus Christ, the Son of God" (Mark 1:1). Matthew records, "Jesus was going throughout all Galilee, teaching in their synagogues and proclaiming the gospel of the kingdom, and healing every kind of disease and every kind of sickness among the people" (Matthew 4:23).

Few things are as simple as the gospel. While thousands of books and academic articles discuss the subject, it remains a simple message to preach and to understand. It is summarized in a single line in Paul's letter to the Romans: "But God demonstrates His own love toward us, in that while we were yet sinners, Christ died for us" (Romans 5:8). That simple message has changed the lives of millions and forever altered the face of history and the future.

Though easy to understand, the gospel doesn't always generate a simple response. Paul wrote to the troubled believers in Corinth, "For the word of the cross is foolishness to those who are perishing, but to us who are being saved it is the power of God" (1 Corinthians 1:18). The message of Christ divides the listening congregation every time. Some immediately recognize the truth of it; others work hard to find fault. The simple message brings about a complex response.

The passage at the beginning of this chapter is a plea for help. After telling the Ephesians they should protect themselves with the armor of God, Paul makes a heartfelt request: "Pray for me." And for what does he seek prayer? Words. Of all the things he could have asked for, he asks for the ability to explain the gospel in a manner that all would understand. It sounds simple, but the situation was difficult.

Paul wrote the book of Ephesians while he was imprisoned in Rome. He knew he soon would have to give an accounting of his faith before Caesar, where he would face accusations from his Jewish opponents. In other words, he would have to explain the gospel to a polytheistic, Roman leader in the presence of Jewish opposition. He could expect trouble from both sides. Rome viewed both Christians and Jews as atheists since they refused to worship Caesar as a god. It also viewed Christianity as a sect of Judaism, while Jewish religious leaders saw this new religion as a heretical threat to their faith.

Paul knew both the Romans and the Jews were mistaken. Jesus had changed all the rules. To make others understand that, he had to open the mystery of the gospel in such a way that they could see the hand of God in it. That was a challenging enough task for a free man. Paul was a prisoner, making the work all the more difficult. He was in a hostile setting, facing opposition before an unsympathetic ruler who had an ax to grind against both sides.

He needed the right words, and he needed all the prayers he could get. Paul's fear was not imprisonment or even execution. He had resolved himself to a life of hardship and the likelihood of martyrdom. His greatest fear was a failing of words.

Paul's concern that he use convincing words reminds me a bit of the rail-thin fellow student I once heard preach when I was a college student. Our school sent out student "evangelism teams" that included student musicians, student music leaders, and a student preacher. Many preachers-to-be received their first experience of public evangelism while serving on these teams. On this occasion, I sat in a pew and listened to this young man plead with the congregation about their need to accept Christ. He lubricated his plea with tears. The church was small and it was an evening service, the time when only the most dedicated came out. There was a good chance that everyone in the room was a believer. Still, the youthful evangelist proclaimed and pleaded, his passion washing over him like a tsunami. Watching him urge people to walk down the aisle made me uncomfortable. Only later would I come to appreciate that his heart was set on making sure that no one left the building without hearing about his or her need for Christ. That young preacher was awkward, disorganized, and had a grating voice—but he was also committed to making sure the Word went out. He had the same drive as the apostle Paul, whose greatest fear was that his words would fail him.

OPEN TO ALL, CLEAR TO SOME

Paul spoke of the "mystery" of the gospel. We have learned that the word *mystery* means something formerly hidden but now unveiled. In that sense, how is the gospel a mystery?

Although Jesus' message is good news, the response to the gospel is not always positive. That is the irony and much of the mystery of the gospel. The response to Jesus, in fact, was always one of division. Some immediately recognized Him as the Messiah—taking in the Good News from the Good Messenger. To others, the religious leaders in particular, Jesus brought "bad news." Their expectations were wrong, their interpretations of the Scriptures in error, and their hopes for the future misplaced. They refused to understand that Jesus was revealing the mystery, unveiling God's plan from the eternal past in their very real moment.

While many religious leaders rejected the gospel outright, others tried to change the gospel, to custom-fit it to their preconceived ideas. From the earliest days of the church many have boldly proclaimed: "We have it right; you have it wrong."

Two such groups were the Gnostics and Judaizers. The Gnostics claimed a special and exclusive knowledge of spiritual matters that one obtained only from them. A person was either in their circle or out of the loop. Not even the apostles had such knowledge, they claimed. The name *Gnostic* comes from the Greek word meaning "to know." For them, knowledge was the key to salvation. They claimed to have the inside scoop. Any knowledge apart from them was incomplete. There were two types of Gnostics. Both believed that the physical (matter) and spiritual were at odds. For one group, that meant denying the flesh as much as possible. The other side taught that what one did in the body had no effect on the soul; therefore, one could live promiscuously. The teachings of the Gnostics were at odds with Christ's message on too many points to number. For them, the simple message of Christ was not enough. Paul and John fought these heretical ideas in their letters to the churches.

The Judaizers were a different problem. They sprang up soon after the founding of the church. On the surface, they appeared as Christian as anyone else did, but there was more to them than met the eye. Their basic premise was that people could not be good Christians unless they were also good Jews. For Jewish believers, this wasn't much of a stretch, but for non-Jewish Christians it was a huge hurdle. Judaizers taught that circumcision, ceremonial washing, and other distinctively Jewish practices were part of the salvation process. In short, they believed that Gentiles had to convert to Judaism before becoming Christians. The teaching sent Paul into a rage. "I wish that those who are troubling you would even mutilate themselves," he said in Galatians 5:12, alluding to their doctrine of circumcision. It was a harsh wish, but the danger presented by the Judaizers was that great. They were teaching that Christ was not enough and that faith alone was inadequate. Nothing could be further from the teaching of the apostles or more dangerous to the church.

The simplicity of the gospel message offended the Gnostics and the Judaizers. Both added requirements that Jesus never intended. Certainly, nothing as important as faith could be so simple, these false teachers thought. Each in its own way compartmentalized the world into "insiders" and "outsiders." To a Gnostic, a person with their special knowledge was an insider. To a Judaizer, only fellow Jews or Jewish converts could be on the inside; no one else belonged.

Not much has changed. Some reject the gospel as foolishness the moment they hear it. Others try to trim it here and there to make it more palatable to their lifestyle. Some balk at the gospel's simplicity; others are uncomfortable with the idea of a suffering Savior. The urge is to make the gospel fit us, like a finely tailored suit, rather than tailoring ourselves to the gospel.

And this leads to the real mystery of the gospel: the criteria for acceptance. While false teachers were running down the apostles and watering down the gospel, God was adding to the church—and He did so without checking passports. The most thrilling aspect of the mystery of the gospel is that it includes everyone regardless of heritage, gender, or lineage. This meant that the Gentiles were welcome. Paul writes, "And this is God's plan: Both Gentiles and Jews who believe the Good News share equally in the riches inherited by God's children. Both are part of the same body, and both enjoy the promise of blessings because they belong to Christ Jesus" (Ephesians 3:6, NLT).

First-century Jews, including Jesus' disciples, were not comfortable with Gentiles. A long and troubled history, compounded by Gentile pagan practice and Roman domination, made it impossible for Jews to feel comfortable about the Gentiles around them. Yet when Jesus came, He welcomed everyone who would believe: fishermen, tax collectors, political zealots, and women (an odd thing in that culture). He helped Jew and Gentile alike, going so far as to say of one Gentile, a Roman army officer, "I say to you, not even in Israel have I found such great faith" (Luke 7:9).

Clearly Jesus planned to include the Gentiles in the Kingdom from the very beginning. Before ascending into heaven, He gave His final command to the disciples. "It is not for you to know times or epochs which the Father has fixed by His own authority; but you will receive power when the Holy Spirit has come upon you; and you shall be My witnesses both in Jerusalem, and in all Judea and Samaria, and even to the remotest part of the earth" (Acts 1:7-8). Jesus made the command in response to the disciples' question, "Lord, is it at this time You are restoring the kingdom to Israel?" (Acts 1:6). They were still letting their long-held expectations cloud their understanding.

These verses serve as an outline for the book of Acts. The message goes out exactly as Jesus lists it here. Jesus was commanding His Jewish disciples to cross over into uncomfortable waters. Geographic borders were not going to be the problem.

They were to begin in Jerusalem, which was where they were when Jesus gave the command. Most of the disciples were from Galilee in the northern part of the country. After His ascension, they were not to return home but to stay in the city until the Holy Spirit came upon them, an event that would happen a little less than two weeks later. From Jerusalem, they were to take the gospel throughout the entire southern part of the country called Judea.

The next geographical region mentioned is Samaria. Samaria is in central Palestine and different from Jerusalem and Judea. Samaritans were descendents of Jews who had married foreigners. That was offensive to strict Jews. Orthodox Jews of the day would have nothing to do with the Samaritans, going so far as to shake the dust from their feet if they had walked on Samaritan soil. It's difficult for people of our era to imagine the shock that the disciples must have felt when Jesus commanded them to preach to the Samaritans. Even then Jesus wasn't done. He added that they should take the good news to the "remotest part of the earth." Clearly, Jesus meant the gospel for the world. That's common knowledge now, but it was astonishing news then.

Even after the church had been around awhile, believers debated the Gentiles' role. The first church council dealt with this very topic. Could Gentiles be saved as Jews could be saved? Peter delivered the definitive opinion at the Council of Jerusalem. Acts 15 records the speech.

> *After there had been much debate, Peter stood up and said to them, "Brethren, you know that in the early days God made a choice among you, that by my mouth the*

*Gentiles would hear the word of the gospel and believe.
And God, who knows the heart, testified to them giving
them the Holy Spirit, just as He also did to us; and He
made no distinction between us and them, cleansing their
hearts by faith." (vv. 7-9)*

We can imagine the church leaders arguing, debating, and
batting the Scriptures back and forth. God had already
decided the matter. Gentiles were not only receiving the
gospel gladly, but they were manifesting the same traits of the
Holy Spirit earlier Jewish believers had, proof that God had
accepted the Gentiles just as He had accepted the Jews. What
that first council had to do was learn what God was doing
and join Him in the work.

Two thousand years later, it seems silly that the debate
took place at all. Yet it was a divisive issue that had to be
addressed before the church could mature into what Christ
intended it to be. The leaders of the church had to come to an
official and public acknowledgement that Jesus established
the church for Jew *and* Gentile alike. Faith knows no nationality. That is part of the mystery of the gospel. It is inclusive
of all who will believe. Birth certificates and pedigree papers
are unnecessary. As Paul, the apostle to the Gentiles, says,
"There is neither Jew nor Greek, there is neither slave nor
free man, there is neither male nor female; for you are all one
in Christ Jesus" (Galatians 3:28).

I was reminded of this recently while attending a minister's
retreat in the mountains of California. The head of a denomination stood at a microphone and called on a pastor to lead
the group of 250 in prayer. He suggested that the pastor pray
in his native tongue. The South American minister prayed in
Portuguese. There I was, watching an African-American man
introducing a South American pastor who prayed over a
group of Anglos, Japanese, Korean, African, Chinese, Viet-
namese, Russian, and others whose heritage stretched
around the world. It struck me that this should be a remarkable act, but no one commented at all. If we had sat in the
first church council, we would have seen people of the same

background and heritage struggling to imagine what we take for granted today.

KINGDOM WITHOUT BORDERS

Only Christ can bring people of all nationalities and backgrounds together. The heart of the gospel—and the Person who unites believers in the Kingdom of God—is Jesus. In his book on God's Kingdom, British theologian Richard Bewes comments that "the ceaseless quest of the human spirit . . . has been for a leader who can command such universal allegiance as to rise above the title of 'The Great' and gain recognition as 'The Only.'"[3]

Tradition says that toward the end of the third century, an army division chose to obey "The Only" at high cost to themselves. Maurice was the leader of the Egyptian Theban Legion, a division of the Roman army. The Theban Legion was composed entirely of Christians. Called to help suppress a revolt in Gaul, Maurice and his men arrived to find that a slaughter had taken place. To his surprise, Maurice soon learned the dead that lay on the battlefield were Christians. The ruler Maximinus ordered the whole army to make sacrifices of thanksgiving to the Roman gods for the success of the campaign. Maximinus had several Christians killed as part of the celebration—it was his cruel way of making a point about Rome's view of Christians. Remembering that Jesus had taught to render to Caesar the things of Caesar and to God the things of God, Maurice and his men refused to make the sacrifices. Although loyal to Rome, they felt a greater loyalty to Christ.

Maximinus ordered a decimation of the Theban Legion— the killing of every tenth man. When that failed to move the others to comply, he ordered a second decimation and another 10 percent were killed. When it was all over, every member of the Theban Legion was executed by beheading, choosing to die rather than make sacrifices to false gods.

Maurice—an African—and his men were just a few of the brave and dedicated believers who held Christ more important than life itself. They understood that they were citizens of a Kingdom without borders. That was a revolutionary concept.

The gospel requires a response to Christ and His Kingdom, something another leader refused to do. History views Pontius Pilate, the Roman governor of Judea, as cruel, ineffective, offensive, and often apathetic. We see this in his face-to-face confrontation with Jesus. It reads like a dialogue in a movie script. The New International Version of the Bible records it this way:[4]

Pilate:
Are you the king of the Jews?

Jesus:
Is that your own idea, or did others talk to you about me?

Pilate:
Am I a Jew? It was your people and your chief priests who handed you over to me. What is it you have done?

Jesus:
My kingdom is not of this world. If it were, my servants would fight to prevent my arrest by the Jews. But now my kingdom is from another place.

Pilate:
You are a king, then!

Jesus:
You are right in saying I am a king. In fact, for this reason I was born, and for this I came into the world, to testify to the truth. Everyone on the side of truth listens to me.

Pilate:
What is truth?

Pilate (to Jesus' accusers):
I find no basis for a charge against him.

It is an amazing conversation. Jesus, already beaten and battered, stood before the only man who could send Him to the cross. Pilate's great concern was insurrection and revolt.

He was under orders to execute anyone claiming to be a king, other than those appointed by Rome. Jesus knew this, yet He refused to be intimidated. In the last hours of His life, He spoke of His Kingdom. In this powerful and poignant moment, Jesus teaches us several things.

First, Jesus tells us that His Kingdom is not an earthly one. That will change in the future, after Christ comes again to set up His millennial reign, and of course He'll rule in the New Heaven and New Earth. For now, His Kingdom is something other than what we can see. Its seat of government is in heaven, not on earth. *Kingdom* was a dangerous word in the first century. Rome tolerated no talk of other kingdoms. It was a capital offense.

Jesus' Kingdom breaks the mold. There are no geographical boundaries, no marker posts. It exists in this world and beyond and encompasses everyone and everything. That's the next thing Jesus teaches in His confrontation with Pilate. Not only is His Kingdom "not of this world," but it "is from another place." Its origins predate time and extend beyond measurable space.

MOUTH-TO-MOUTH RESUSCITATION

Another aspect of the mystery of the gospel is its role in expanding the Kingdom. History shows that all great empires began with conquest. One nation overtakes and occupies another. It's an ancient pattern. Armies amass and then march on their neighbors: seizing land, enslaving people, and overthrowing governments.

The Kingdom of Christ expands by conquest as well, but not in the usual sense. It isn't by might but by right that the Kingdom of God grows. The gospel is "good news," a "great report." At its core is the idea of broadcast. The word spreads. News isn't news unless someone announces it. Here is another facet of the mystery of the gospel: Christ has entrusted His servants to take the greatest news in the universe to the world. From our mouth to someone else's ear, it continues. After noting in his letter to the Romans that whoever calls upon the Lord will be saved, Paul says, "How then will they call on Him in whom they have not believed? How will they believe in Him whom they have not heard? And how will they hear without a preacher? How will they preach unless they are sent? Just as it is written, 'How beautiful are the feet of those who bring good news of good things!'" (Romans 10:14-15).

Police detectives speak of chain of custody. The term describes the process by which evidence moves from one place to another—from crime scene to evidence locker to the forensics experts to court. In a sense, we are part of the chain of custody for the gospel. We are not just the *recipients* of grace; we are the *bearers* of it. Peter tells us to "sanctify Christ as Lord in your hearts, always being ready to make a defense to everyone who asks you to give an account for the hope that is in you, yet with gentleness and reverence" (1 Peter 3:15). Ready, willing, and able, as they say in the military.

Every conversion to Christianity is the result of a chain of faithfulness. Whether we came to Him under someone's preaching, or by the sharing of a friend, or even through a book or article, we can ultimately trace our salvation back to Jesus' command to the disciples to "go and make disciples" (Matthew 28:19, NLT). From the very beginning, believers have known that the church is one generation away from extinction. Jesus has trusted us to tell others of what we have come to know as truth. That's the mystery of the gospel.

JOINING THE DIPLOMATIC CORPS

The apostle Paul asked for prayer that he might have the right words to say in defense of the mystery of the gospel. That simple request reminds us of our responsibility to live and to speak the Good News.

In 1966, a translation of the New Testament called *Good News for Modern Man* came out in paperback. It was easy to read and made understanding the Bible much easier for new believers. It was my first Bible, and the title has always intrigued me. Good News from the past is Good News for the present. That is the essence of the gospel. Modern man needs the same truth first-century believers did. We are a part of that, the product of an unbroken chain of faithful witness, and that same truth now rests with us. By action, by word, and by prayer we carry the message for others to see and hear. That makes each of us an ambassador.

An ambassador is someone who represents one government to another. We have seen that one facet of the mystery of the gospel is that there exists a Kingdom open to all in faith, a Kingdom that knows no boundaries and cannot be marked off by borders. The Christian has a visible, earthly existence as well as a spiritual citizenship in an unseen Kingdom. Although we are born in this world, in a sense we are foreigners, with a spiritual nationality.

The gospel is good news for the hearer and the bearer. It changes lives today as thoroughly as it did 2,000 years ago. It is good news received and then passed on. We hold the cure for spiritual disease. We present it simply, honestly, and openly, and others respond.

Good news for ancient man.

Good news for modern man.

Good news—period.

Paul asked the pressing question, "How will they believe in Him whom they have not heard? And how will they hear without a preacher?" (Romans 10:14). That is a valid question. We have been empowered by the gospel to become children of God; we are entrusted with the gospel to make sure that others have the same opportunity.

FOR REFLECTION

1. Describe the meaning of the word *gospel.*
2. Why do you think the gospel often causes controversy, even though it is clear to Christians that it is "good news"?
3. What are some aspects of the "mystery of the gospel"? (See Acts 1:8; 15:7-9; Galatians 3:28; and Ephesians 3:6.)
4. What did Jesus mean when He told Pilate, "My kingdom is not of this world"?

5. On page 158, the authors say, "We are not just the *recipients* of grace; we are the *bearers* of it." Describe some ways in which you might be a messenger of the gospel in your everyday life.

CHAPTER 13

The Mystery of the Church

It is absolutely essential that a church perceive itself as an institution for the glory of God. JOHN F. MACARTHUR
The Master's Plan for the Church

This mystery is great; but I am speaking with reference to Christ and the church. EPHESIANS 5:32

T*HEY just don't get it.* How many times do
we read a Gospel account of the disciples' interactions with
Jesus and wonder at their continuing ignorance and unbelief? Not long after watching Jesus multiply five loaves and
two fish into a feast for five thousand, the disciples panicked
when Jesus told them to feed four thousand people who'd
spent three days listening to Him preach. Just after Jesus
privately told His twelve disciples about His upcoming death
and resurrection, James and John asked Jesus if they could
sit in the places of honor in His coming Kingdom. So often
those closest to Jesus seemed to miss the point.

Perhaps that explains Jesus' unbridled joy to Peter's
response when He asked his disciples, "Who do people say
that the Son of Man is?" (Matthew 16:13). It's a question easy
to answer now, but one that required real insight at the time.
The disciples began to list a series of answers: "Some think
you're a prophet like Elijah or Jeremiah, others think you're
John the Baptist." After all this time, people were still
confused about the person of Jesus.

Then Jesus pressed the question and He made it personal:
"But who do you say that I am?" (v. 15). That was a different

question. This pop quiz may have unsettled some of the disciples. There could be no hedging, and taking the "party line" was out. After a moment's silence, Peter laid it on the line: "You are the Christ, the Son of the living God."

"Blessed are you, Simon Barjona, because flesh and blood did not reveal this to you, but My Father who is in heaven," replied Jesus. "I also say to you that you are Peter, and upon this rock I will build My church; and the gates of Hades will not overpower it. I will give you the keys of the kingdom of heaven; and whatever you bind on earth shall have been bound in heaven, and whatever you loose on earth shall have been loosed in heaven" (Matthew 16:16-19). While joyfully affirming Peter's confession, Jesus was also revealing the mystery of the church, the representative of His Kingdom on earth.

What made Jesus respond with such utter joy? First, Peter's assertion came from personal experience, not hearsay, not influenced by the opinions of others. "Flesh and blood did not reveal" this to Peter. The source of the understanding was none other than God. That was the importance of the question. While others debated what kind of prophet Jesus was, Peter had finally come to understand that Jesus was the Christ, the Messiah, which meant that He was more than any man. The Old Testament taught the Jews of Jesus' day that the Christ would be divine (Isaiah 9:6; Jeremiah 23:5-6; Micah 5:2).

To proclaim that Jesus was the Christ was no small statement. In fact, it was a dangerous one. Peter used the Greek term the *Christ* (*ho Christos*), a word that was similar to the Old Testament *messiah*. The terms carry the idea of the One anointed of God and in whom God would fulfill all His promises. The title *Christ* also carried political baggage. In a world ruled by Rome there could be only one leader, Caesar. Romans might understand a public admission that Jesus was "the Anointed One" as treason. That didn't matter to Peter. Jesus was who He was and Peter said so.

This was not the first time anyone put two and two together. Nathanael confessed, "Rabbi, You are the Son of God; You are the King of Israel" (John 1:49). Before that,

Andrew found his brother Simon Peter and declared, "We have found the Messiah" (John 1:41). After this event, Peter stated, "We have believed and have come to know that You are the Holy One of God" (John 6:69). And after staring death in the face during a vicious storm that Jesus calmed with a single phrase, the disciples said, "You are certainly God's Son!" (Matthew 14:33). But each of those confessions was made after the disciples witnessed a miracle. Peter made his confession in response to a direct question, not in the staggering awe that followed a supernatural event.

This was not an emotional answer but one based on an intellectual and heartfelt understanding. Peter elevated Jesus above every prophet by calling Him the Christ and raised Him above humans by calling Him the Son of the Living God. This very belief would lead to Peter's martyrdom. Paul, all but one of the disciples, and countless Christians through the ages would also die for the same belief. The statement was more than a collection of words meant to tickle Jesus' ears. It was a solid, heartfelt connection.

Not only did Jesus praise Peter for his faith, He made it clear that His church would include those who made the same confession that Peter voiced. Though the word *church* is familiar and used often in the New Testament, Jesus uses it only three times and on only two occasions—less than 3 percent of the times the word appears in the New Testament.

The Greek word *ekklesia* means a gathering of people, those called out for a purpose. The word appears 118 times in the New Testament, and 115 of those refer to a body of believers (the other three times the word is translated "assembly" or something similar). Ironic, isn't it? The founder of the church almost never used the word, but after His death and ascension, it became one of the most frequently used terms in the New Testament.

Scholars have wrestled over Jesus' intended meaning: "I also say to you that you are Peter, and upon this rock I will build My church; and the gates of Hades will not overpower it." This is a debated passage. The trouble is rooted in a play on words. "Peter" means "rock" in both Aramaic (the spoken language of the day) and Greek (the preferred written language). Jesus then uses the word to refer to the foundation upon which He would build His church. There is a difference worth noting. Peter is written, as we would expect, in the masculine; "rock" is in the feminine. The words refer to different types of rocks. *Petros* indicates a stone, a pebble, or a piece of some large rock. *Petra* indicates something large and firm, like a ledge jutting from a cliff or bedrock.

Jesus isn't saying that He will build His church on Peter, but on the truth behind Peter's confession—in other words, on Himself. We can imagine Jesus pointing at Peter and saying, "You are a rock," then indicating Himself and uttering, "Upon this bedrock, I will build My church." The New Testament echoes this concept. Paul said, "For no man can lay a foundation other than the one which is laid, which is Jesus Christ" (1 Corinthians 3:11). This does not minimize Peter's importance. He would be the church's first pastor. In most evangelical churches, Peter receives too little admiration, in others too much.

What makes this passage more meaningful is its context. Jesus had retreated from primarily Jewish territory into the mountainous Gentile area. Caesarea Philippi was approximately twenty-five miles north of the Sea of Galilee and snuggled at the foot of the Mount Hermon mountain range. At one time, it had a different name: Panion. It was called that because of a cave-sanctuary dedicated to the worship of the Greek god Pan. In Old Testament times, people worshipped the false god Baal in the area. Herod the Great built a marble temple to Caesar Augustus there. Jesus and the disciples stood in an arena of dead gods—manufactured deities—that crossed several cultures. Amidst these surroundings, Peter proclaimed Christ as the Son of the living God. Peter understood.

The real thrust of the passage is that it is Jesus who builds His church and that the church would be anchored to His nature. Jesus is the beginning, middle, and end of all things, especially the church. Here is where the mystery begins.

Ancient Judaism was irrevocably tied to Abraham and his descendents. It was an ethnic faith with global influence.

People took great pride in their ability to trace their lineage back to the father of the Jews. Luke traces Jesus' line back to Adam! (Luke 3:23-38). Jesus is revealing the next step in the plan: He would build a church, one founded on the people's relationship with Him, not on a genetic tie to Abraham.

The church would do more than exist—it would charge the gates of Hades. Often Matthew 16:18 ("the gates of Hades will not overpower it") is used to portray the church withstanding an attack from hell. This is wrong on several counts. First, the word used is *Hades*, not *hell*. *Hades* is the New Testament term for the Old Testament word *Sheol*. It is the abode of the dead. Hell is a place of *future* punishment. Second, it is the church on the attack, not Hades. Jesus chose His words carefully: "gates of Hades." Gates are not offensive weapons; they are defensive. They have only two purposes: to keep what is outside, out; and to keep what is inside, in. The image is of the church charging the gates of hades and kicking those gates down. In other words, the church will change the whole institution of death.

Death could not hold Christ. He rose from the dead and so will every believer. This helps us understand Jesus' next comment about the church: "I will give you the keys of the kingdom of heaven; and whatever you bind on earth shall have been bound in heaven, and whatever you loose on earth shall have been loosed in heaven" (Matthew 16:19).

Rendering thoughts and statements from one language to another is a tricky business. Translating New Testament Greek into twenty-first-century American English can be slippery work. The languages differ greatly, and often the ancient Greek is complicated. Most English renderings of these words would have us believe that whatever we as a church (or Peter specifically) bound here, God would bind in heaven and whatever we let loose, He would also loosen.

Several translations have tried to make the English as literal as the Greek. The result is an accurate but awkward-to-read rendition of the Scriptures. Dr. Kenneth Wuest did such a work in the early 1960s, called the *Expanded Translation*. His goal was to use as many English words as necessary to get the biblical idea across to the reader. He translates Matthew 16:19 this way: "I shall give to you the keys of the kingdom of heaven; and whatever you bind on earth [forbid to be done], shall have been already bound [forbidden to be done] in heaven; and whatever you loose on earth [permit to be done], shall have already been loosed in heaven [permitted to be done]."[1]

The perfect tense of the verbs makes us realize that heaven is not following our lead; we're following heaven's. As Warren Wiersbe says, "Jesus did not say that God would obey what [the disciples] did on earth, but that they should do on earth whatever God had already willed. The church does not get man's will done in heaven; it obeys God's will on earth."[2]

Jesus is being frank and descriptive. He would hand the gospel over to His followers: to the disciples first, then to the new church and down through the ages until it rests with us. This is one of the differences between the church and what came before. The church is to be heavenly minded, outwardly concerned, and not just introspective. The church is in the world-changing business. "God rules the world and His Church through the prayers of His people," says Andrew Murray. "That God should have made the extension of His kingdom to such a large extent dependent on the faithfulness of His people in prayer is a stupendous mystery and yet an absolute certainty."[3]

The disciples were the first to hear about something new under the sun: the church, founded, fueled, and sent by Christ. The world had never seen anything like it. Through persecution, poverty, and rejection, it has taken the keys given it by Jesus and done its work. Keys either open or lock. Christ has entrusted the eternal unchanging message of His love, His salvation, His forgiveness, and His sacrifice to the church. Every day, the church, this gathering of called-out ones, changes the face of the world and of heaven.

ADMISSION REQUIREMENTS

We are a visual people tending to judge what is by what we see. In most cases, that is a good policy, but some things go beyond the obvious. When asked who belongs to the church, we tend to look around our church sanctuary and identify those we see each Sunday. Church goes far beyond a street address. Although the debate about mode of baptism, local church government, service times, and worship styles continues, one thing is certain: The church Christ founded has no walls, no physical address, no denominational title, no conventions, or home office. The "church universal" extends beyond physical boundaries and even the margins of time.

To join a local church, you might be required to walk down the aisle in a Sunday service, fill out a form, or perhaps go through a membership class. These are good things. No criticism should be leveled at a local church that strives to raise up educated and eager servants for Christ. Not only is the local church important, it is a vital component of Christ's work on earth. The local church is the physical, tangible, temporal representative of the universal church. The local church makes headway with the gospel, provides a place of worship, teaches doctrine, ministers to believers, reaches out to unbelievers, and introduces Christ to the world. The apostle Paul spent his life establishing local churches. He paid a dear price doing so. The local church has always had and continues to have great influence in the world. It will be that way until Christ comes again.

Yet the key to understanding the mystery of the church is to remember that it is less an organization and more an organism. The invisible church is a beautiful mystery frequently missed. Still the universal church is not a place or a local set of believers. It includes believers of all the ages who have placed their faith and trust in Christ. We belong to the same church as the apostles, the first deacons, the first missionaries, and the first Christians.

It is interesting to see how the Bible refers to the church. More often than not, the biblical writer addresses the congregation not by where they meet, but by where they live. "To the church of God which is at Corinth," Paul writes, "to those who have been sanctified in Christ Jesus, saints by calling, *with all who in every place call on the name of our Lord Jesus*

Christ, their Lord and ours" (1 Corinthians 1:2, emphasis mine). Note the connection Paul draws between the believers in Corinth and those elsewhere in the world. He wrote to "the saints who are at Ephesus" (Ephesians 1:1) and "to the church of the Thessalonians" (1 Thessalonians 1:1). In Peter's first epistle, he faced a different problem. Persecution had driven Christians from jobs and homes and from the cities of their birth. Still, he addressed them as a single organism and wrote "to those who reside as aliens" (1 Peter 1:1).

WE, THE HOLY CONDOMINIUM

Until AD 70 when it was destroyed, the Temple in Jerusalem was one of the most admired buildings in the world. Gold covered the interior, and spacious courtyards surrounded the 150-foot-tall stone building. It covered thirty-six acres marked off by a massive wall. It took decades for King Herod to make all his ambitious alterations that continued even after his death. Final work was finished in AD 64–six years later the Romans would destroy it, razing it to the ground.

Inside the Temple was the Holy of Holies, a thirty-foot-by-thirty-foot room in which the ancient Jews believed God dwelt. The ancient Jews didn't believe that God was confined to the gold-plated room, but that He manifested Himself there in ages past. Paul calls that image to mind when he asked, "Do you not know that you are a temple of God and that the Spirit of God dwells in you?" (1 Corinthians 3:16).[4]

Part of the mystery of the church is the organic, unbreakable bond between Christ and the institution for which He died. Paul phrased it as, "Christ in you." Jesus indwells His church, as does the Holy Spirit. God the Father does the same. In a sense, the church is a holy condominium. This connection is unique in history. While God separated out a people for His name, while He promised them a land of their own, while He blessed them during their great periods of obedience, He was seen as above the nation of Israel or dwelling in the Temple.

The church enjoys the benefit of being the temple in which God, Jesus, and the Holy Spirit dwell. This intimacy sets the church apart from any institution in history. The connection between Christ and His church cannot be broken or even frayed. Local churches may part from God, may even die in place, but the unseen, universal church to which every Christian belongs lives on through eternity.

This understanding puts life into the church; it also should cause serious reflection about what we do, say, value, and how we project the truth of Christ in our churches. It is an important matter to be part of the church.

Perhaps you've had the experience of being out of town and visiting a vital church. You join in the worship; you speak with the people and find that you feel strangely at home, even though you have never before met any of the other attendees. Belief makes us relatives through Christ—we have the same salvation experience, value the same faith, and worship the same God. That connection makes us family, and we are comfortable with family.

When I look out over a congregation, I feel a different sensation than when I'm at a play looking over the audience. Not long ago, I sat in the Kodak Theater in Hollywood waiting for one of my favorite musicals to start—Andrew Lloyd Webber's *Joseph and the Amazing Technicolor Dreamcoat.* The theater was buzzing as patrons worked their way down the aisles and to their seats. I was enjoying myself. The Academy Awards had been held there and I wondered which star or producer or writer had sat where I was sitting that night. I stood to stretch my legs and surveyed the theater. A wide mix of people were there and we all had something in common—our appreciation of Sir Andrew's plays. Still, something was missing. While I shared an interest with these people, I didn't sense that I shared an eternity with them. When I speak at Christian gatherings or churches, I feel a bond with strangers. That bond is Christ.

BODY LANGUAGE

One thing every human can relate to is the human body. After all, we each have one. Of the many metaphors used in the Bible to describe the mystery of the church, Christ's body

is perhaps the most vivid. In his letter to the church at
Corinth, Paul wrote a chapter portraying the gifts given by
the Spirit. The gifts vary as much as humans do, so he drills
into them the point that many members make one body.
"Now you are Christ's body, and individually members
of it," Paul instructs in 1 Corinthians 12:27. He says something similar to the church in Rome: "For just as we have
many members in one body and all the members do not have
the same function, so we, who are many, are one body in
Christ, and individually members one of another" (Romans
12:4-5).

Paul's emphasis is the believer's use of spiritual gifts for the
good of the church, but he also intended for us to understand
that believers are as tightly connected to one another as
fingers are to a hand, feet to legs, and lips to face. All are
important, all have a place, and all have a purpose. Every
believer is a functioning part of the church—the body of
Christ. Of course, the head of the body is Christ Himself. All
that we do is in support of Jesus.

Our society tends to see in either/or colors, greater or
smaller degrees, important or less important functions. Big
churches are seen as more "successful" than small churches,
large Sunday schools as more powerful than smaller ones,
and pastors of megachurches as more admired than country
church parsons. Logically, we know all that is nonsense, yet
the comparisons persist. In some churches, pastors, deacons,
trustees, elders, and others are viewed as more important
than other members. It was never meant to be so. The illustration of the body puts such false ideas to rest. Anyone who
has ever had a broken toe knows what a seemingly insignificant body part can do. Those who have had amputations tell
us how difficult it is to adjust, even if the lost body part is a
finger or toe. While life can go on without a toe or a leg or an
eye, the body's function is diminished.

That is the beauty of the church—every believer is needed;
every believer has a role to perform and a part to play. All are
equal in the church. The division between laity and clergy is
artificial. We all stand before Christ as sinners made clean; as

offenders declared innocent. In that sense, we are all the
same and no amount of skill or money changes that standing.
However, we are gifted in different ways, with the Holy Spirit
imparting to each of us some skill that benefits the church.
For some, those skills are in administration; others in teaching; others in preaching; and others in evangelism. No one is
gifted in all things, and that is by plan. We fit a part, a sche-
matic designed by God. That plan allows people of different
skills, backgrounds, and education to work in tandem,
complementing the efforts of others.

One of the greatest mistakes the local church can make is
to expect the pastor to be administrator, teacher, counselor,
preacher, evangelist, and janitor. It is an unfair expectation
that disappoints the congregation and frustrates the pastor. It
is also contrary to the procedures of Christ. All of these roles
are important, but no one person can be expected to fulfill
them all.

The question is never: "What should others be doing?" but
"What should I be doing?" This is one of the most liberating
facets of the mystery of the church. Everyone has a place;
everyone contributes. Just as we value every part of our
bodies, so Christ values each of us.

MIXING METAPHORS

One of the first things writers learn is not to mix metaphors.
A metaphor is a literary sleight of hand in which one thing is
compared to another. It's considered bad form to use too
many metaphors or combine them in a single thought.
Phrases like "When the chips are down, I'll back you to the
hilt" are confusing and jarring.

Concern over metaphors is a recent one. Paul had no problem blending two different visual ideas into the same
thought. He did it in a passage about husbands and wives that
is also about Christ and the church. In Ephesians 5:23-32, he
writes:

> *For the husband is the head of the wife, as Christ also is*
> *the head of the church, He Himself being the Savior of the*

body. But as the church is subject to Christ, so also the wives ought to be to their husbands in everything.

Husbands, love your wives, just as Christ also loved the church and gave Himself up for her, so that He might sanctify her, having cleansed her by the washing of water with the word, that He might present to Himself the church in all her glory, having no spot or wrinkle or any such thing; but that she would be holy and blameless.

So husbands ought also to love their own wives as their own bodies. He who loves his own wife loves himself; for no one ever hated his own flesh, but nourishes and cherishes it, just as Christ also does the church, because we are members of His body. "For this reason a man shall leave his father and mother and shall be joined to his wife, and the two shall become one flesh."

This mystery is great; but I am speaking with reference to Christ and the church.

The church is Christ's bride. The church is Christ's body. Why the mixed metaphor? Because no single illustration can fully describe the church and Christ's eternal relationship to it. We are related to Him as well as organically connected to Him. More than one description is needed to help us understand the organization that reaches from heaven to earth and that spans the eternal past to the eternal future. No single comparison or illustration can describe the love Jesus has for His church, so we see the church as Christ's bride, wife, body, gathered ones, set-apart ones, and more.

Paul wanted it made clear to all believers that the relationship between Christ and the church is the highest-level connection, very much like the relationship between husband and wife. While teaching the Ephesian church the value of marriage and the mutual submission of husband and wife (wife to her husband; husband willing to die for his wife), Paul—ever the teacher of doctrine—couldn't resist folding in some other important information.

First, Christ is the head of the church. Not many would dispute that. The word Paul uses for head (*kephale*) can refer to the literal head of a person or animal. Interestingly, it is also used in a Greek verse that is translated "chief corner-stone"[5]–another metaphor for Christ and His church.

Second, we see that Jesus is the "Savior of the body." The idea of *savior* is that of a rescuer, one who comes to the aid of another in mortal danger. Jesus is certainly that. He snatched us from death. That is the basis for the often-used Christian term "saved." Those in the church were once in a life-threatening situation but Jesus snatched them out of harm's way.

Next, Paul shows us that Jesus is to the church what a husband is to a wife–more specifically, to a bride. Then as now, a bride was the center of attention at a wedding. There's a beautiful thought here. Of all the possible illustrations he might have used, the husband-wife one is most comforting. Jesus doesn't view His people as slaves, employees, or as mere pieces of a puzzle–they are family, joined by a spiritual marriage, and like a perfect husband, He cares for them and is even willing to die in their place. Beyond that, He has worked to perfect His bride "so that He might sanctify her, having cleansed her by the washing of water with the word, that He might present to Himself the church in all her glory, having no spot or wrinkle or any such thing; but that she would be holy and blameless" (Ephesians 5:26-27).

Sanctified means "to be set apart for some task." In the days of the Temple, certain items and furnishings could only be used in the Temple. They belong to God and had been set apart for His worship. Today we borrow tables and chairs from our local church, but no one could borrow a table or candle stand from the Temple. Jesus has sanctified His church, setting its members apart from the world and for Himself.

He also has cleansed His church by the washing of water with the Word. This isn't a reference to baptism but to the prenuptial cleansing a bride would undertake before her wedding. The goal of all of this was to present us, His church, in glory and perfection, which isn't something the church or the individual could do on his or her own. In this marriage metaphor, the bridegroom makes everything possible, and the washing we receive frees us from the stain of sin and makes it possible for us to be sanctified, separated for Christ's purposes.

Paul then makes a touching observation. Husbands are to "love their own wives as their own bodies." The lesson for the church today is to remember that we are involved in a love relationship with Jesus. So often, we see Jesus as maintaining a long list of our faults and failings; of scrutinizing every move, every thought; of shining a bright light on our lives searching for blemishes. While we should be concerned with our behavior and attitudes, we do a disservice to Jesus by portraying Him as a spiritual boogeyman looking for a reason to punish us or at least remove His blessing.

"Greater love has no one than this, that one lay down his life for his friends. You are My friends if you do what I command you. No longer do I call you slaves, for the slave does not know what his master is doing; but I have called you friends, for all things that I have heard from My Father I have made known to you" (John 15:13-15). Doesn't sound like a vindictive Savior, does it? Friends, not slaves, Jesus called us; friends with whom He shared the mystery of the gospel; friends for whom He showed the greatest love by dying for them—for us.

The beautiful mystery of the church is that it is rooted not in law, not in restrictions or code of conduct, but in a love relationship that supersedes all others. Jesus' love for us—for you—compelled Him to go to the cross to die; our love for Him compels us to live for Him.

THE CHURCH ALL CAUGHT UP

Of the mysteries involving the church, one garners more attention than any other. The Rapture—the snatching away of believers at some point before Christ's second coming—has been the subject of books, debates, and even bitter argument. For some, it represents a whole line of end-times thinking that they find uncomfortable. Others make it a central part of their doctrine. Either way, two passages make it clear that something significant is going to happen to the church in the future.

The first passage is nestled at the end of one of the most important sections of the Bible. First Corinthians 15 is meant to end any doubts about the resurrection of Christ. No issue is more important to the Christian faith than Christ's resurrection. Each spring, churches around the world celebrate Easter because it is the keystone of our faith. So important is the Resurrection that Paul bluntly states: "For if the dead are not raised, not even Christ has been raised; and if Christ has not been raised, your faith is worthless; you are still in your sins. Then those also who have fallen asleep in Christ have perished. If we have hoped in Christ in this life only, we are of all men most to be pitied" (1 Corinthians 15:16-19).

It makes us shudder. If Christ is not risen then we have no hope for the future, death is permanent, our faith is useless, and we are left as little more than empty shells to be pitied by others. But the best news of all is that Christ did rise from the dead, did make twelve appearances, and showed Himself to hundreds of people. In His resurrection is the promise of our own bodily resurrection.

Paul adds, "But now Christ has been raised from the dead, the first fruits of those who are asleep" (1 Corinthians 15:20). Mentioning first fruits implies there will be second fruits. As Christ was raised, so every believer will be resurrected. You and me, raised to bodily life at some time in the future. When? We don't know. While we may not know the date and hour, the Rapture speaks of that event for the church.

First, a word about the word *rapture*: it does not appear in the Bible. It's a coined term, one meant to call to mind a concept larger than the word itself. We can say the same thing about the term *Trinity*, which appears nowhere in the Bible. *Rapture* is an English term used to carry the meaning found in the Greek word *harpazo*: to catch away, snatch, pluck, and to seize. The word may not appear in the Bible, but the teaching does.

Paul, in the midst of his discussion on the vital importance of Christ's resurrection, shifts gears to discuss the resurrection of the believers. "Behold, I tell you a mystery;" he writes, "we will not all sleep, but we will all be changed, in a moment, in the twinkling of an eye, at the last trumpet; for the trumpet will sound, and the dead will be raised imperishable, and we will be changed" (1 Corinthians 15:51-52). These verses are loaded with information.

First, Paul calls this event a mystery. He is unveiling to the church what has been unveiled to him—the hidden laid out in the sunlight. Just as Christ was raised, so shall we be, but in an unexpected way. "We will not all sleep." It's an odd phrase. Early Christians, especially the apostle Paul, referred to death as sleep, a euphemism for what occurs to those who died. (This should not be confused with the erroneous concept of "soul sleep," the concept that the dead "sleep" waiting for Christ's return, an idea with no biblical support.) Many Old Testament passages say that the deceased "slept with his fathers," meaning that person had died. Paul reveals that death is not an end, is not permanent, and is not something that should worry Christians: The soul of one who has died flourishes with God and will be reunited with its body in the resurrection.

The trumpet shall sound to announce the glorious moment when the dead are raised imperishable and forever changed. The key here is where we the church meet Christ. To learn that, we must examine another statement by Paul. To the church in Thessalonica Paul writes:

> But we do not want you to be uninformed, brethren, about those who are asleep, so that you will not grieve as do the rest who have no hope. For if we believe that Jesus died and rose again, even so God will bring with Him those who have fallen asleep in Jesus. For this we say to you by the word of the Lord, that we who are alive and remain until the coming of the Lord, will not precede those who have fallen asleep. For the Lord Himself will descend from heaven with a shout, with the voice of the archangel and with the trumpet of God, and the dead in Christ will rise first. Then we who are alive and remain will be caught up together with them in the clouds to

> *meet the Lord in the air, and so we shall always be with*
> *the Lord. (1 Thessalonians 4:13-17)*

Concern over the grief churning in those early Christians fueled Paul's words. Everyone dies. Most everyone witnesses death at some time. It is never pleasant and hearts broke then as they do now. During the first quarter of the second century, a man named Aristides described the Christian response to death. "If any righteous man among the Christians passes from this world, [his fellow believers] rejoice and offer thanks to God, and they escort his body with songs and thanksgiving as if he were setting out from one place to another nearby."[6] It is an admirable and realistic description, but grief is still a normal response, even for Christians. Early Christians shed tears just as modern believers do.

Paul felt the need to comfort them and teach a truth with which they could comfort one another. His approach was to give information about the future. He didn't want them to remain in ignorance. Knowledge changes the possessor and truth enables the believer. In this case, knowing that not only is there life beyond death but that every believer will be resurrected was comforting to anyone who had lost a loved one. It didn't remove the grief but made it manageable by bathing the heart and soul in hope. Paul encouraged those ancient brethren not to grieve like those who had no hope.

His argument began with a confession common to Christians: Christ died and rose again. Then he laid out the events: The Lord will appear and the dead in Christ will rise. Those believers who are alive at the time will then be "caught up" together in the clouds. This last detail is fascinating. Many have argued against the catching away of the believers by saying, "I believe in only one Second Coming." They are right to believe so. The Bible shows only one return of Christ, but the Rapture, the catching away of the believer, is not the Second Coming but the "First Going." A distinction is made between the saints being caught up to meet Christ in the air and the physical return of Christ to the earth. When Christ returns, He does so with "*all* His saints" (1 Thessalonians

3:13, emphasis mine), those believers who previously met Him in the air.

This is a future event for the church and one of the revealed mysteries. A time will come when the church will be removed from the world. Many scholars believe this will happen before the Tribulation described by Jesus (Matthew 24:21) and shown in Revelation.[7] It may be the very act of removing the church from earth that enables the Tribulation, a seven-year period of severe judgment and persecution that will immediately precede Christ's second coming, to happen.

One of the most beloved passages of Scripture, which is frequently read at funerals, is John 14:1-3. "Do not let your heart be troubled; believe in God, believe also in Me. In My Father's house are many dwelling places; if it were not so, I would have told you; for I go to prepare a place for you. If I go and prepare a place for you, I will come again and receive you to Myself, that where I am, there you may be also." This passage portrays lovely mansions built by the Savior. It's an image worth holding, but equally impressive is Jesus' promise to "receive" us to Himself so that we may be where He is. Jesus used the word "receive," which means to take alongside, to bring together, to move to a close proximity. What He describes here is not His second coming but our catching away at the Rapture.

One of the mysteries of the church is the way in which Christ will bring His bride to His side, an event yet to happen and one believers look forward to with eager anticipation.

THE PLACE FOR IMPERFECT PEOPLE

The great revelation of the church is that it has a perpetually open door. Many shy away from the church because they expect to find merely a pretty, steeple-adorned building filled with people who live just this side of perfection. How different their view would be after just a few visits to a Bible-centered congregation. Instead of Nice Ned and Perfect Patty, they would find folks just like them, people working their way through life, enjoying the adventures or enduring the hardships. The difference is what enables them to persevere through life. The Christian sees everything in this world as somehow related to his or her service to God. The good, the bad, the tragic may be beyond our comprehension, but we know the one who understands.

Church has always been the place for imperfect people, which is good since that is the only kind of people in this world. More hospital than hotel, more home than country club, the local church is the visible representation of the universal church, the place for those who serve Christ. It is the place where seekers search and searchers seek. From the beginning, it has been the tool Christ has used to reach those for whom He died.

Martyn Lloyd-Jones says, "We must cease to think of the Church as a gathering of institutions and organizations, and we must get back the notion that we are the people of God."[8]

The church is the great equalizer. Background, wealth, education, past sins, and troubled questions are all set aside while Christ is worshipped. Jew and Gentile become one; male and female stand in equality; young and old face the same eternal life. That is the mystery of the church—it came in an unexpected way, piloted by unexpected men and empowered by the Holy Spirit to do more than any man or woman imagined. "The Church is a society of sinners," Charles Clayton Morrison is reported to have said, "the only society in the world in which membership is based upon the single qualification that the candidate shall be unworthy of membership."

Church is still the place for people of faith, sinners that we all are. For people of faith, it remains home.

FOR REFLECTION

1. Why was Jesus so pleased at Peter's confession of faith in Matthew 16:16?
2. What do we learn about the church in Jesus' response to Peter?

3. While Judaism is tied to Abraham and the covenant, to whom is the church tied? How?

4. Describe how the marriage relationship illustrates Christ's relationship to the church.

5. What is the future of the church?

6. What misconceptions about the church have you heard from family members or friends? Based on what you've read in this chapter, how might you respond the next time one of them raises an objection about church or the people who are part of it?

CHAPTER 14

The Mystery of Israel

*God did entrust the descendants of Abraham with the first
revelation of Himself.*   C. S. LEWIS

*For I do not want you, brethren, to be uninformed of this
mystery—so that you will not be wise in your own estima-
tion—that a partial hardening has happened to Israel until the
fullness of the Gentiles has come in.*   ROMANS 11:25

I N 2004, Mel Gibson, actor and director, released a movie that created great controversy and fear. *The Passion of The Christ* set records at the box office. It also got people talking. Before the first frame flickered on the big screen, critics attacked the movie, which graphically shows the betrayal, torture, and crucifixion of Jesus. The great fear? Commentators feared the movie would ignite a new wave of anti-Semitism. Some felt that Christians would turn on Jews and label them "Christ killers." They feared violence and reprisal. While there may have been isolated cases, the concerns of widespread anti-Semitism proved unfounded. Still the anxiety was real and highlighted a myth that refuses to die: that Christians hate Jews.

Most Christians recognize the nonsense of such a statement. Although there have been hate groups that have taken the name of Christ and used it to justify illegal and unbiblical actions, Christians are quick to point out that not only do we not hate the Jews, we are indebted to them. Craig Keener observes, "Gentile racism against Jewish people is as contrary to the focus of Christianity as Jewish prejudice against Gentiles; racism of any sort opposes the message of the gospel."[1]

Christianity has deep Jewish roots. No true believer can be anti-Semitic. The Savior is Jewish, born to a Jewish mother, lived in a Jewish home, ate Jewish food, lived on Jewish land, spoke Hebrew and Aramaic, and performed His first earthly miracle at a Jewish wedding. Further, He delivered His message to the Jews first, chose Jewish men to be His disciples, and entrusted them with the greatest message of all time. Jesus was distinctly Jewish, but His message crossed every human barrier. Believers grounded in the Bible know that Jesus went to the cross to pay for our sin—every person's, whether Jewish or Gentile.

Still this idea persists along with another invalid concept—that God is done with the Jews, that He has written them off and replaced them.

What is the place of Israel in God's scheme of things? Does the nation still fit into God's plan or has He erased it from the future? These are very contemporary questions but they're not new. Humans are pendulums, swinging from one extreme to another. In the first century, a group of Jewish believers called Judaizers believed that Gentiles must first become Jews before they could be proper Christians. On the reverse side of the coin were those who thought Judaism was dead, having committed spiritual suicide through its choice of unbelief.

The answer is less complex than most imagine and is found in the Epistles, where God reveals the "mystery of Israel."

A MYSTERY ALL SHOULD KNOW

Paul wrote many of the books of the New Testament. Inspired by God, he penned his words with great purpose and razor-sharp logic. He was not one to waste time or resources. The book of Romans is a great example of this. Paul filled the letter with deep, doctrinal teaching, including a powerfully written explanation of Israel's place in God's plan. And Paul wrote those words to correct a growing misunderstanding.

Paul states his desire for his readers to understand an important reality. He writes it in the negative, "For I do not want you, brethren, to be uninformed of this mystery." There are two types of confusions: not knowing (simple ignorance) and misunderstanding (believing bad information or misconstruing good information). The church at Rome was composed of Gentile and Jewish believers. Their upbringing made them suspicious of each other. In Christ, they were supposed to lay such suspicions aside, but humans find it difficult to remove a coat of prejudice they've been wearing all their lives.

The Jews had to wonder if their role as a nation had been set aside for the Gentiles, whom they had been taught were spiritually inferior. Some Gentiles, on the other hand, began to feel superior to the Jews, especially after hearing from Paul and others that the nation of Israel had rejected the gospel message. Paul had to put the matter to rest, and the only way to do so was to educate them about God's plan. Chapter 11 of Romans is that lecture, given in writing. To understand the mystery of Israel, we must first understand what Paul taught.

Paul begins by using himself as an example. "I say then, God has not rejected His people, has He? May it never be! For I too am an Israelite, a descendant of Abraham, of the tribe of Benjamin" (Romans 11:1). He emphatically states the conclusion before he lays out his argument. God has not rejected His people. End of discussion. Then with ethnic pride, he reminds the Roman Christians that he, too, is Jewish and proud of it. These must have been refreshing words to the Jewish believers and a strong reminder to their Gentile brethren. In beautiful ancient rhetoric, Paul asks a question in such a fashion that it demands a "no" answer. Paul did not cease to be Jewish the day he gave his life to Christ. His lineage and history remained important to him. It made him who he was.

Then Paul makes an example of Elijah, a powerful prophet whose ministry took a personal toll. After repeated confrontations with Israel's king Ahab and his wife, Jezebel, Elijah was depressed and emotionally beaten. He complained to God: "I have been very zealous for the Lord, the God of hosts; for the sons of Israel have forsaken Your covenant, torn down Your altars and killed Your prophets with the sword. And I alone am left; and they seek my life, to take it away" (1 Kings 19:10). We can reduce Elijah's argument to a single phrase: "There's nobody left who believes but me."

Elijah was wrong, and God told him so. "Yet I will leave 7,000 in Israel, all the knees that have not bowed to Baal and every mouth that has not kissed him" (1 Kings 19:18). Elijah was not alone. He may have *felt* alone. He might have imagined himself alone. But God could name 7,000 people who had refused to bow and kiss the idol Baal, even though the reigning king and queen had demanded that they do so. John Witmer says, "God was not limited to one fearful, depressed prophet; He had reserved for Himself a godly remnant in Israel that numbered 7,000. The preservation of the faithful remnant was a work of God."[2] Elijah was wrong–although we can certainly sympathize with the great man–to assume that God had waited until there was only one believer left in Israel. The first-century Christians were equally mistaken to think it was impossible for Jews to believe or that God had given up on them. God had a remnant of believers then as He did in Elijah's day: "In the same way then, there has also come to be at the present time a remnant according to God's gracious choice" (Romans 11:5).

So what then was the problem? Paul puts it this way, "What then? What Israel is seeking, it has not obtained, but those who were chosen obtained it, and the rest were hardened" (Romans 11:7). Two things stand out like a neon light: Israel was seeking something it had not obtained, and some of the Jews were hardened.

What was Israel seeking? They sought what all spiritually hungry people seek: acceptance by God. Their system for pleasing God was adherence to the Mosaic law and its many human amplifications. Still, the fact that Israel was in rebellion when Christ came is not a Gentile idea. The religious leaders who so often challenged Jesus believed that the people had wandered away from the law and its many requirements. The Sadducees felt their Jewish brethren were wrong about resurrection, angels, and which books of the

Old Testament had authority. The reclusive Essene felt the
nation was so far off the spiritual beam that they withdrew
from society entirely and founded strict religious communi-
ties.

The rebellion of the nation was no secret. This is one
reason why so many wanted Jesus to set up an earthly kingdom above all else, and why so many were disappointed that
He didn't conform to their wishes. However, all of these
groups misunderstood the purpose of the law. It could not
save God's people; its purpose was to prove that people
cannot earn salvation, it comes as a gift from God.

Paul had already highlighted this for the Romans when he
wrote, "For what the Law could not do, weak as it was
through the flesh, God did: sending His own Son in the likeness of sinful flesh and as an offering for sin, He condemned
sin in the flesh, so that the requirement of the Law might be
fulfilled in us, who do not walk according to the flesh but
according to the Spirit" (Romans 8:3-4).

In other words, the Jews had to understand that the law,
although given by God, was not the means of salvation. The
Gentiles needed to learn that it was impossible to earn salvation by making sacrifices to gods who didn't exist. Salvation
was something brought about by Christ alone. Salvation by
grace had always been the plan of God. Faith is the key that
unlocks that grace, even in the Old Testament. (See Hebrews
11.) This was difficult for Jewish believers to embrace. It
went against centuries of teaching by their leaders, even
though it was clearly taught in the Old Testament. Just as
there were Jews who became disciples of Christ, there were
Jews around the world who would receive the teaching of
Christ. That hasn't changed over the centuries.

Yet some Jews refused to believe, and as a result their
hearts were made unresponsive to God's truth. The concept
of God hardening someone's heart is awkward for most of us.
It seems unfair, out of character, and just plain un-Godlike.
How can God harden someone's heart, especially when we
understand that the word means to blind, make callous, or
even to petrify? Why would He do that to the very group of

people He singled out as special? Hardening is the result of a choice not to believe or apply what should be believed. It occurs when a person is repeatedly insensitive to God's word and His call. To see this we need look no further than the Gospels.

The Gospel of Mark records two surprising events in which the hearts of the disciples were hardened. First, Mark 6:51-52: "Then He got into the boat with them, and the wind stopped; and they were utterly astonished, for they had not gained any insight from the incident of the loaves, but their heart was hardened." This is the account of Jesus walking on the water. The disciples had witnessed and participated in the feeding of a large, hungry congregation. Jesus took a few fish and loaves and multiplied them to feed a crowd of five thousand men (meaning the actual numbers may have been closer to twelve thousand to fifteen thousand). When suddenly faced with danger, the disciples' faith evaporated as if blown away by the winds of the storm. What they had seen hours before didn't seem to apply. It was impressive and remarkable, but not something they took to heart. It is amazing to see the word *hardened* here in reference to the disciples. The disciples were Jesus' confidants, helpers, and believers, yet their hearts were hardened because they had not appropriated the truth.

Mark records another event that happened after the feeding of the five thousand and the feeding of the four thousand, two seemingly unforgettable events. The ministry team of Jesus encountered another food shortage—their own. While on a boat trip across the Sea of Galilee, they noticed that they had only one loaf of bread, not nearly enough for a boatload of grown men. For some reason, they could not understand that Jesus could do for twelve what He had done for well over nine thousand men and accompanying women and children.

Mark 8:17-21 recounts it this way: "And Jesus, aware of this, said to them, 'Why do you discuss the fact that you have no bread? Do you not yet see or understand? Do you have a hardened heart? Having eyes, do you not see? And having ears, do you not hear? And do you not remember, when I broke the five loaves for the five thousand, how many baskets full of broken pieces you picked up?' They said to Him, 'Twelve.' 'When I broke the seven for the four thousand, how many large baskets full of broken pieces did you pick up?' And they said to Him, 'Seven.' And He was saying to them, 'Do you not yet understand?'"

Again, Jesus mentions their hardened hearts, and again we are astonished to hear these words used in reference to the men who would change the world through their faith.

Years ago, I sat in my office at the church where I served as pastor when a woman came to see me. "I want to talk to you about your sermons," she said. My stomach turned. No good conversation begins that way. "I feel your preaching is far too negative," she explained. "We need to hear more about God's love and forgiveness; more about joy and happiness. You need to stop being so negative, Pastor." Feeling confident that she had now put me on the right course, she left. The next day a man made an unscheduled stop by my office. He sat in the same chair as the woman. "Pastor," he began, "I've come to talk to you about your preaching." More stomach gymnastics and I steeled myself for what was to come. "Your preaching is far too positive. We need to hear more about sin, God's righteousness, the judgment to come, and our need for confession. You're just tickling the ears of the congregation. I don't feel like I've worshipped unless I leave a little beat up." Confident he had set me straight, he left. It was difficult to walk into the pulpit that next Sunday. I knew that no matter what I preached, one of the two was going to be unhappy.

Same message but different responses. These two parishioners had heard the same words, but drew different conclusions. Each had a set of expectations that I wasn't meeting, and if I succeeded in meeting the one, I would be offending the other. It was a lose-lose situation. The only solution was to preach the biblical text and not worry about what others thought.

John recorded the critic's chosen response: "But though He had performed so many signs before them, yet they were not believing in Him" (John 12:37). Jesus uttered these words in the face of frustrating, persistent, chosen disbelief. No matter how many miracles He worked, no matter how many signs and wonders He performed, there were those who refused to believe.

While individuals did indeed turn to Christ in faith, the nation did not. Jesus said their hearts were hardened just like in Isaiah's day. It was a result of choice. They saw what they wanted to see; they heard what they wanted to hear. The ancient Jews had a set of expectations that God wasn't meeting. This is not a Jewish trait; it's a human trait.

In the book of Isaiah we gain an interesting insight into "heart hardening." Isaiah's call to ministry was one of the most dramatic and visual of any in the Bible. Isaiah 6 records a vision the prophet had of the throne room of God. He saw things certain to bring any man to his knees: seraphs (a type of multiwinged angel), smoke, and most astonishing of all—God on His throne. The chapter records Isaiah's initial response: "Woe is me, for I am ruined! Because I am a man of unclean lips, and I live among a people of unclean lips; for my eyes have seen the King, the Lord of hosts" (Isaiah 6:5).

Seeing God, hearing the angels shout, "Holy, Holy, Holy is the Lord of hosts," would unsettle anyone. In a symbolic act, God cleansed Isaiah, qualifying the prophet to be God's spokesman. God then called Isaiah to a ministry of frustration and failure. He would receive the message from God and faithfully proclaim it, only to have it rejected repeatedly. What is intriguing is the provocative way God describes what Isaiah would do. "Go, and tell this people: 'Keep on listening, but do not perceive; keep on looking, but do not understand.' Render the hearts of this people insensitive, their ears dull, and their eyes dim, otherwise they might see with their eyes, hear with their ears, understand with their hearts, and return and be healed" (Isaiah 6:9-10).

Render the hearts of this people insensitive? Isaiah's message would not only demonstrate the calloused hearts of the people, but it would contribute to it. Here is the understanding we've been searching for: Hard hearts are the result of decisions we make. When Moses went toe-to-toe with Pharaoh, he knew the king would not budge. God had told him as much. Exodus tells us that three times Pharaoh hardened his own heart.[3] Only then, did God directly harden the Egyptian king's heart.

As with the disciples, Pharaoh, and the people of Isaiah's day, a hard heart is the result of sin, disobedience, and a refusal to respond to God's direction. Today the viewer of Internet pornography might feel awash in guilt and remorse the first time he yields to the temptation to view lewd pictures, only to find the remorse and repentance dissolving a bit more each time he returns to look at the photos again. The more one sins, the easier it becomes to do. Rejecting the message of Christ thickens the heart, dulls the spiritual hearing, and blinds the eyes. The disciples experienced this when they refused to see that miracles were not magic tricks but demonstrations meant to bring about trust in Christ.

The message of Christ always gets a response. God would harden the hearts of Isaiah's people simply by presenting them with the truth. Each rejection added a layer to the cataracts on their spiritual eyes. Israel had a history of acceptance and rejection. When Jesus presented Himself as the Son of Man, Son of God, and Messiah, He forced a national choice. As a nation, the Jews chose to deny all that they heard, to write off every miracle seen, to ignore every one of the scores of prophecies in the Old Testament. In every case the result was a heart hardened against truth.

Does this mean that Israel has no place in God's plan, that He has divorced Himself from the people He called and set apart and with whom He made a covenant? No. The disciples experienced heart hardening, but Jesus didn't send them packing. Indeed, they became His ambassadors to the world.

Paul taught the Romans that a partial hardening had occurred and that God was working through the Gentiles, but he also made an impassioned argument demonstrating that God remains faithful no matter how unfaithful His chosen nation may be.

ISRAEL OF OLD, ISRAEL OF NOW

Romans 11 is Paul's defense of Israel's importance. He acknowledges that as a nation they have rejected the Messiah, but he also builds a solid case that they continue to play an important role in God's plan. He also makes it clear that Gentiles have no right to lord their new spiritual position over the Jews, reminding his readers that Gentile believers are believers because God raised up Israel and many Jews became followers of Christ. To use Paul's metaphors, the nations are the branches connected to the tree trunk of Israel; they are wild olive branches grafted onto the cultured olive tree.

The psalmist says, "For the Lord will not abandon His people, nor will He forsake His inheritance" (Psalm 94:14). In the age of grace, God uses the church as His means of bringing the lost to salvation. Some have even assumed that the church has replaced Israel, but that is not the case. Israel is irreplaceable. It had and continues to have a role to play in prophetic history. Others have tried to prove that the church is the New Israel, with the former tossed away and now supplanted. This fails to match the teaching of Scripture. The Lord has not and will not abandon His people.

In explaining this to the Romans, Paul writes, "From the standpoint of the gospel they are enemies for your sake, but from the standpoint of *God's* choice they are beloved for the sake of the fathers; for the gifts and the calling of God are irrevocable" (Romans 11:28-29, emphasis mine). During Paul's day, the first great persecution of the church came from the Jews. Paul knew that; he was one of the chief persecutors. Later, the Romans would take Paul's life and attempt to annihilate the fledgling church. Still fresh in the minds of many Christians was the persecution that began in Jerusalem and spread to nearly every city with a significant Jewish population. In that sense, Israel was the enemy of God and the church. But as Paul explained, God's viewpoint is balanced with past successes and great Israelites.

In the Old Testament, God had entered into a legal contract with Israel called a covenant. A covenant is a simple agreement between parties. Some covenants bind both parties to a prescribed behavior. For example, God made a conditional covenant with Moses and Israel. "Now then, if you will indeed obey My voice and keep My covenant, then you shall be My own possession among all the peoples, for all the earth is Mine; and you shall be to Me a kingdom of priests and a holy nation" (Exodus 19:5-6). A conditional covenant binds both parties to some action. God said, "If you will indeed obey My voice and keep My covenant. . . . " The agreement was valid as long as Israel kept its part of the bargain. But God also obligated Himself. If Israel was faithful, then God would make them His possession (meaning that He would exalt them above other nations) and they would be a kingdom of priests, a holy nation like none other.

But God also entered into unconditional covenants in which He promised to do or not to do something without putting stipulations on the other party. The covenant with Noah is a good example. God promised to never again curse the ground or flood the earth. He placed no requirement on Noah or his descendents.

God made another unconditional covenant with a man in the ancient city of Ur. His name was Abram, soon to be Abraham. "Now the Lord said to Abram, 'Go forth from your country, and from your relatives and from your father's house, to the land which I will show you; and I will make you a great nation, and I will bless you, and make your name great; and so you shall be a blessing; and I will bless those who bless you, and the one who curses you I will curse. And in you all the families of the earth will be blessed" (Genesis 12:1-3).

This is what Paul has in mind when he wrote, "but from the standpoint of God's choice they are beloved for the sake of the fathers; for the gifts and the calling of God are irrevocable" (Romans 11:28-29). God repeats this covenant several times through the generations. God honors His covenant.

The nation of Israel rejected Jesus, but God has not rejected Israel. The world is blessed through them and a time will come when "all Israel will be saved" (Romans 11:26). *Saved* (*sozo*) means to remove from danger, to protect, to heal, and to preserve. In this verse, Paul is not saying that everyone in Israel will be spiritually saved. Salvation is not a national decision but an individual one. He is saying that in God's plans for the future, the nation of Israel will be preserved and restored to its proper spiritual condition. Most likely, Paul has in mind the thousand-year reign of Christ on the earth (see Revelation 20:1-6).

GOD'S CHOICE, GOD'S CALLING

Israel did reject the Messiah and that decision proved costly. They had been offered the opportunity to fulfill all that God had meant for them, but hard hearts—hardened first by themselves and then by God—made it slip through their fingers. It was a grievous decision that has had a negative impact on their society through the centuries. But God's plan cannot be thwarted by intention or omission. The message of God's love has gone out through the Gentiles, something that has been a blessing to them.

Salvation is through Christ and Christ alone. Salvation does not come by ethnic connections, genetic similarity, or common history. As Peter said in one of his early sermons, "And there is salvation in no one else; for there is no other name under heaven that has been given among men by which we must be saved" (Acts 4:12). No other name—a fact that time cannot change.

It would be a mistake, however, to think that the New Testament has disposed of the people of God. Paul's point in the mystery of Israel chapter is that Israel is now and will forever be part of God's program. Paul says it this way, "I say then, they did not stumble so as to fall, did they? May it never be! But by their transgression salvation has come to the Gentiles, to make them jealous" (Romans 11:11). Paul previously told the Roman congregation, "And we know that God causes all things to work together for good to those who love God, to those who are called according to His purpose" (Romans 8:28). While the Jews of Jesus' day rebelled, God used it to the benefit of the world.

OF DISOBEDIENCE AND MERCY

As mentioned earlier, the ancient world was prone to divide the world into "them" and "us." That human tendency continues. In some ways, it is an accurate representation, but instead of seeing the world as black and white, Jew and Gentile, we see the world as saved and unsaved. Paul, using himself as an example, writes, "It is a trustworthy statement, deserving full acceptance, that Christ Jesus came into the world to save sinners, among whom I am foremost of all. Yet for this reason I found mercy, so that in me as the foremost, Jesus Christ might demonstrate His perfect patience as an example for those who would believe in Him for eternal life" (1 Timothy 1:15-16).

Patience. God is patient, holding off wrath in favor of blessing. His desire is to see each person come to Christ, but He knows (as we all do) that many will turn away. Disobedience is a privilege granted to individuals and nations. God remains the ultimate second chance. The roller-coaster history of the Jews is evidence of God's great mercy. Several times His judgment fell upon His people, but only after repeated warnings and years of patience. Each time, Israel returned to its land and its standing.

Israel holds a special place in God's program and always will. That special standing makes their rebellion against Christ so hard to understand. Yet no one can cast the first stone. Gentiles reject Christ as well. The Romans worked hand in hand with the Jewish conspirators to crucify Jesus. Romans took persecution to the highest level the world has ever seen.

Israel's place in God's plan may be interesting, but what does it say to us? We have the same choice Israel had. We can accept Christ or deny Him. The ancient Jews had many prophecies to show that Christ was who He said He was; we have the Bible that does the same and more. God is not finished with Israel, nor is He finished with the rest of us. As ancient Israel, even when led by godly kings, sometimes failed God, so do individual believers today. In many ways,

Israel is an object lesson for us. Often we wish to say that they are without excuse—the same can be said of us.

Paul, who shows us Israel's failure and then reminds us that God is still at work in that nation, was balanced in his teachings. Early in Romans he takes on the pagan unbeliever, saying that God has made Himself known through creation and that they, the Gentile pagans, are wrapped up in futile speculations with foolish and darkened hearts (see Romans 1:20-23).

Israel's problem is one common to all people. Unbelief is a choice and all choices carry consequences for good or bad. No group can look down its nose at the nation of Israel and say, "You should have known." Yes, they should have, and so should we. "God had chosen Israel as His covenant people from eternity past," John Witmer said, "and entered into a relationship with them that will never be destroyed."[4]

GOD'S COVENANT WITH YOU

In the early 1990s, Bill McCartney, then head football coach for the University of Colorado, helped found Promise Keepers, a nonprofit corporation with the dream of uniting men across all cultural and ethnic barriers and inspiring them to keep their promises to God and family. The organization grew with amazing speed. Their first meeting in 1990 consisted of seventy-two men. The next year 4,200 men gathered for worship and encouragement. In the mid 1990s more than two million men attended gatherings across the country.

Keeping one's promises doesn't seem like a novel idea but as Promise Keepers proved, people are drawn to the idea of being faithful to one's commitments. Our God keeps His promises. He always has, and there's no reason to expect anything different in the future. The mystery of Israel teaches us that God is not fickle or whimsical when it comes to covenants He has made. The mystery of Israel is about a nation that rejected the One they should have received. Jews and Gentiles choose between obedience and rebellion every day.

God has made a covenant with you through Jesus. In an upper room two thousand years ago, Jesus broke bread and called it His body, poured wine into a common cup and said, "Drink from it, all of you; for this is My blood of the covenant, which is poured out for many for forgiveness of sins" (Matthew 26:27-28). He wrote this contract in blood and showed it to the world from the height of a cross—and that covenant is as binding today as the day Jesus made it.

God has kept His covenants, including the ones with Israel. Jesus has kept His covenants with the individual believer.

What shall we do with our end of the bargain? Each day is a new opportunity to say, "I believe; I accept; and I will live like it." If God is a promise keeper, we should be too.

God is not finished with Israel, that is the mystery of Israel. God isn't finished with us, either.

FOR REFLECTION

1. Define anti-Semitism. Why is anti-Semitism among Christians so illogical (not to mention wrong)?
2. Why were Christ and His teachings such stumbling blocks to so many of His fellow Jews?
3. Has God rejected Israel? Which Scriptures support your answer?
4. What does the Bible mean by "heart hardening"?
5. How was the nation of Israel's rejection of Jesus as Messiah good news for the Gentiles?
6. What can you as an individual believer learn from God's faithfulness toward the Jewish people? What does it tell you about His attitude toward you?

CHAPTER 15

The Mystery of Lawlessness

There is going to be an ultimate anti-Christ, one person, able to do such wonders that he almost deceives the elect themselves.

MARTYN LLOYD-JONES

For the mystery of lawlessness is already at work; only he who now restrains will do so until he is taken out of the way. Then that lawless one will be revealed whom the Lord will slay with the breath of His mouth and bring to an end by the appearance of His coming; that is, the one whose coming is in accord with the activity of Satan, with all power and signs and false wonders, and with all the deception of wickedness for those who perish, because they did not receive the love of the truth so as to be saved. 2 THESSALONIANS 2:7-10

SOME phenomena are hard to ignore. They demand attention. From time to time, our moon passes between the sun and the earth, casting a shadow that moves across the face of our planet. If you are in the right spot at the right time, the entire sun seems to disappear behind a dark disk. The daylight fades into twilight and, in some cases, the day becomes dark enough that the stars can be seen sparkling above. Something like that gets noticed. So much so, that it is hard to take note of anything else–hence the term *eclipse.*

In the Bible, there are passages that make a comment or teach a truth so profound that we overlook important details. The classic example of this is John 3:16. "For God so loved the world, that He gave His only begotten Son, that whoever believes in Him shall not perish, but have eternal life." This is such a powerful statement, and is such a concise description of Jesus' work, that verse seventeen often goes unnoticed: "For God did not send the Son into the world to judge the world, but that the world might be saved through Him." That verse contains additional insights that make it far too important to overlook.

Second Thessalonians 2:7-10 is another example. This

passage addresses the mystery of lawlessness and, ironically, it contains two mysteries. The first, the concept of lawlessness, is the type of mystery that we've been discussing in this book—a truth previously hidden but now revealed by God. However, it is eclipsed by a subject that demands first notice: the Antichrist. Specifics surrounding the coming Antichrist, who will be a leading figure in the end times, are a mystery in the truest English sense—details we don't know.

There is nothing wrong with studying passages that deal with end-time issues. God put them in the Bible for a reason. Such study, carefully made, can yield great information and reveal how God will work in the future. However, it is easy to become so caught up in speculation about the end times that what God has revealed to us goes unnoticed.

Paul addressed these topics to the Thessalonians for a specific reason. He had founded this church less than two decades after Christ's death. As its founder, he naturally felt a close bond with the people. Such bonds can be painful when the objects of our love are suffering. That was the case with this church. Soon after establishing a church there, Paul had to flee for his life to the city of Berea. He wrote two letters to the congregation he left behind. In them, he dealt with two problems.

The first difficulty was the persecution the believers faced, and Paul spoke of their "perseverance and faith in the midst of all your persecutions and afflictions which you endure" (2 Thessalonians 1:4). The exact nature of the persecutions is unknown, but it was real and pressing. Because of this abuse, the church was troubled from without, but they also were bothered from within. A false teaching had arisen, perhaps from some flavor of Gnosticism. Someone was teaching the church that the congregation had missed the second coming of Christ. It is easy to imagine how upsetting that would have been: "Now we request you, brethren, with regard to the coming of our Lord Jesus Christ and our gathering together to Him, that you not be quickly shaken from your composure or be disturbed either by a spirit or a message or a letter as if

from us, to the effect that the day of the Lord has come"
(2 Thessalonians 2:1-2).

Interesting words are in these verses. The idea that they
had somehow missed the Second Coming had shaken them
to their souls. Paul encouraged them not to "be quickly
shaken" from their composure. *Shaken* is the word used to
describe earthquakes, storms, and other violent activities.
Composure is the word for calmness, especially of the mind.
F. F. Bruce translates the clause: "We beg you not to be
quickly shaken out of your wits."[1] That is an accurate and
picturesque way of putting it. Paul tells them not to be rattled
by this false teaching. Jesus had not forgotten them.

He also urged them not to be "disturbed." The original
word comes from a term that means "to cry aloud, to wail."
The first phrase refers to the sudden shock of the news; the
second to the ongoing response. It's unsettling to think of the
reaction of these poor people, still young in the faith, when
they heard that Jesus had come and gone, leaving them
behind in a world that was persecuting them for their faith.
How anxiously they must have waited while news of the
disturbance traveled the many miles to Paul, who was then in
Corinth. It would take time for Paul to write his thoughtful
reply and weeks for the epistle to be delivered to the church.
It was a long and nerve-racking time.

A PAST EVIL

The popular scholar Herschel Hobbs writes, "One should
approach this passage humbly and with an admission of a
lack of understanding."[2] It isn't often scholars begin a
commentary with a disclaimer, but if ever one was needed it
is here in 2 Thessalonians. The passage deals with a past and
future problem. In the midst of that is the lesson of the
mystery of lawlessness.

The early church was born in a world of spiritual upheaval
that ranged from the strict worship of the one God to the
pervasive polytheism of Rome. Into this mix came the Christian church, which strict Jews rejected and Rome persecuted.
Under Nero, Christians on crosses lined the streets of Rome.

The horror of being fed to wild beasts or being crucified, stoned, beheaded, pummeled, or run off were always possibilities for early Christians. It was a hard life.

Yet when we read the apostles' response to such persecution, we quickly see that they expected such treatment, as well they should have. Jesus kept nothing back from His disciples. As early as the Sermon on the Mount in Jesus' teachings, He said, "Blessed are those who have been persecuted for the sake of righteousness, for theirs is the kingdom of heaven. Blessed are you when people insult you and persecute you, and falsely say all kinds of evil against you because of Me. Rejoice and be glad, for your reward in heaven is great; for in the same way they persecuted the prophets who were before you" (Matthew 5:10-12).

Blessed means "to be happy." Jesus' words must have been jarring. Be happy when insulted, persecuted, spoken ill of? How can one be happy under such circumstances? Jesus had more to say on the matter: "These things I have spoken to you, so that in Me you may have peace. In the world you have tribulation, but take courage; I have overcome the world" (John 16:33). Jesus promised peace in tribulation, not an exemption.

The apostles did not shy away from the truth. Paul says, "And not only this, but we also exult in our tribulations, knowing that tribulation brings about perseverance" (Romans 5:3). The book of 1 Peter went to Christians who had been scattered by harassment. Peter taught them to rejoice nonetheless.

Under the emperor Nero, Christians became the scapegoats for the fire that burned Rome in AD 64. He persecuted Christians cruelly, feeding some to lions at gladiator matches and setting others afire to use as torches during his garden parties. Other emperors were no friendlier. At times, to be a Christian meant the sacrifice of property and even life. As God's children living in a fallen world, it should come as no surprise that where there is great good, there often is great evil.

Evil first appeared in the Garden of Eden. In that idyllic

setting, in a place that had yet to see sin, a creature appeared and started a conversation that changed the world. Genesis 3 records the events.

> *Now the serpent was more crafty than any beast of the field which the Lord God had made. And he said to the woman, "Indeed, has God said, 'You shall not eat from any tree of the garden'?"*
>
> *The woman said to the serpent, "From the fruit of the trees of the garden we may eat; but from the fruit of the tree which is in the middle of the garden, God has said, 'You shall not eat from it or touch it, or you will die.'"*
>
> *The serpent said to the woman, "You surely will not die! For God knows that in the day you eat from it your eyes will be opened, and you will be like God, knowing good and evil."*
>
> *When the woman saw that the tree was good for food, and that it was a delight to the eyes, and that the tree was desirable to make one wise, she took from its fruit and ate; and she gave also to her husband with her, and he ate. (vv. 1-6)*

No one can say for certain who the serpent was, although general opinion is that it was Satan or a creature under his power.[3] The serpent's speech is revealing and practiced. It begins with a question, "Has God said . . . ?"; continues with defiance, "You surely will not die!"; and finally moves forward with an accusation, "God knows . . . that your eyes will be opened." All of this shows a *reasoning* tempter. The serpent lies in wait, initiates contact, and attempts to change God's words, implying that He has hidden and selfish motives. To what end? What does the serpent hope to gain? Surely the creature, if he knew as much about God as is implied, knew that punishment would follow. So what was the purpose?

The serpent was a spoiler. His plan was not to gain but to take, to deprive God of something precious. To our knowledge, God had given only one law at that time: "From any tree of the garden you may eat freely; but from the tree of the knowledge of good and evil you shall not eat, for in the day that you eat from it you will surely die" (Genesis 2:16-17). From that command came the possibility of obedience and service, as well as the opportunity for rebellion. Adam and Eve ate of the forbidden fruit, and lawlessness came to humanity.

The mystery of lawlessness is that evil not only exists but that it wages war with God. We have already seen the work of Satan in the Kingdom parables of Matthew 13. The parable of the soils portrays him as birds that eat some of the seed. In the parable of the tares, he sows the counterfeit grain. From the beginning of human history (and probably before that), Satan has opposed all that God is and does. While the world likes to portray him as a goateed man in a red suit with small horns atop his head, he is far worse, far more sinister, and far cleverer. He is a driven creature, consumed by the destruction of all that is holy. Too often, we underestimate him. "For where God built a church, there the Devil would also build a chapel," Martin Luther observed.

Not only is Satan driven, but also he works with skill and purpose. Two passages show this. Paul wrote the church in Corinth, urging them to forgive a repentant sinner within that church "so that no advantage would be taken of us by Satan, for we are not ignorant of his schemes" (2 Corinthians 2:11). The last word is important. *Schemes* is translated from the Greek word for "mind" or "thoughts." Satan works with planning and with forethought, and he has from the beginning.

In another passage Paul says: "Put on the full armor of God, so that you will be able to stand firm against the *schemes* of the devil. For our struggle is not against flesh and blood, but against the rulers, against the powers, against the world forces of this darkness, against the spiritual forces of wickedness in the heavenly places" (Ephesians 6:11-12, emphasis mine). This reference to *schemes* comes from a different Greek word, *methodeia*. Its meaning includes the idea of craftiness and strategy.

The mystery of lawlessness is in those passages. Both the church as a whole and individual believers are engaged in a battle—a war that has been fought throughout time. An end will come, but not until the full plan of God is finished. To be part of the Kingdom of God is to be part of its army.

When Paul brings up the mystery of lawlessness, he does so in the present tense. It "is already at work," he writes. Only then does he go on to future things. Before he does, he introduces another character who has caused great debate. "Only he who now restrains will do so until he is taken out of the way" (2 Thessalonians 2:7). When we watch the news on television or read the newspaper, it is hard to imagine things being worse. Wars, cruelty, and self-centeredness make a mockery of the word *civilized*. Yet, hard as it is to believe, we live in a restrained world.

Many have argued about who this restrainer is. Some see it as Paul's work among the Gentiles; others see it as the Roman government. The most likely person is the Holy Spirit.

The Holy Spirit does His work in the world. Jesus gave a brief outline of that work in His last-minute lesson to the disciples in the upper room. "And He, when He comes, will convict the world concerning sin and righteousness and judgment; concerning sin, because they do not believe in Me; and concerning righteousness, because I go to the Father and you no longer see Me; and concerning judgment, because the ruler of this world has been judged" (John 16:8-11). It is God's act of kindness to keep the world from becoming as bad as it could become. The Holy Spirit restrains humankind and Satan's influence over the world.

Once, in the days of Noah, humanity's morals had plummeted so far that God was compelled to rain down judgment on them. "Then the Lord said, 'My Spirit shall not strive with man forever, because he also is flesh; nevertheless his days shall be one hundred and twenty years'" (Genesis 6:3). This verse is not stating the maximum age a person could live; rather, it refers to the length of time mankind had to change its ways, even as Noah was preparing the ark so he and his family could weather God's judgment on the rest of the world. When taken in context of the ever-rising rebellion, sin, and violence of Noah's day, it seems clear that God was allowing a grace period of 120 years.

Despite God's grief over the world at large, the Bible says, "Noah was a righteous man, blameless in his time; Noah walked with God" (Genesis 6:9). High praise. There's a lot of meaning packed into "blameless in his time." The implication is that he and his family were the last righteous people on the planet. The world had presumed upon God too much and for too long. The judgment of God kicked in.

When we think of that judgment, the first thing that comes to mind is the rising, crashing floodwaters, but judgment began when God decided that His Spirit would not abide in or continue to be at odds with the desires of men. He would remove His Spirit from the world, allowing evil men to become as evil as they wished to be. The restraining work of the Spirit would cease for a time. Lawlessness would grow unchecked.

Why connect Noah to the mystery of lawlessness? Because it is a lesson from history that reflects the future; and because Jesus' second coming is linked to the removal of the church from the world. Jesus put it this way: "For the coming of the Son of Man will be just like the days of Noah. For as in those days before the flood they were eating and drinking, marrying and giving in marriage, until the day that Noah entered the ark, and they did not understand until the flood came and took them all away; so will the coming of the Son of Man be" (Matthew 24:37-39).

Left to our own devices, humanity slides toward evil. Some argue the point and highlight all the great achievements of humankind. Those shouldn't be overlooked, but neither should man's capacity for inhumanity to man. We have crossed over the threshold into the twenty-first century, but the level of crime is no better (and probably worse) than the last century or the century before.

Some of the worst violence seen in the last century happened in 1994. Up to one million Tutsi died in Rwanda. Two tribes, the Tutsi and the Hutu, had been at each other's throats for years. When the presidents of Rwanda and neighboring Burundi died in a suspicious airplane crash, accusations flew like feathers in the wind. Rwandan Hutus, fearing loss of control, turned on Rwandan Tutsis in an effort to wipe out the entire race. The bodies of the murdered, most hacked to death with machetes, choked the rivers. After the fact, many Westerners were sickened by the violence and puzzled by the racial animosity, especially since most could not tell the difference between the Hutus and the Tutsis.

Prejudice among Hutu and Tutsi was the basic problem, but it was made worse by the government's instability. Belgium had granted Rwanda independence in 1961. Problems had reached the boiling point in the last years of Belgium's oversight. In the void of authority left when they pulled out, old hatreds surfaced and evil boiled out of the caldron.

The Holy Spirit is the Restrainer. He prevents the world from sliding down the slope of unchecked evil. That is not to say that humankind is exempt from the malevolence in its hearts. History teaches otherwise. Still, if you can imagine a world without the restraining work of the Holy Spirit, you have an idea of what the Great Tribulation will be like.

A FUTURE EVIL

From a human perspective, lawlessness began with the serpent in the Garden and Adam and Eve's sin of disobedience. The introduction of sin led to their expulsion from the Garden. Sin entered the world. One of the tragedies of sin is that its results are often greater than the sum of its parts. Cain killed Abel and murder came to the world. Sin continued to multiply until it reached such proportions that God destroyed all human life except Noah and his family. It was a clean start, but sin resides in humankind. Lawlessness began anew and continued to grow, prompting Paul to speak of the "mystery of lawlessness" already at work.

He writes, "Then that lawless one will be revealed whom the Lord will slay with the breath of His mouth and bring to an end by the appearance of His coming; that is, the one whose coming is in accord with the activity of Satan, with all power and signs and false wonders, and with all the deception of wickedness for those who perish, because they did not receive the love of the truth so as to be saved" (2 Thessalonians 2:8-10).

The reference to the "lawless one" is what catches most readers' attention, and most scholars agree that Paul is referring to the Antichrist. Paul never uses the term *Antichrist*, but the apostle John does several times. There is a great deal of speculation about the details of the rise and fall of the Antichrist. Most serious Bible students take a cautious but respectful approach to future events. We have few details but enough to make clear the reality of the events.

Jesus revealed some details to His disciples one day as they left the Temple grounds with its scores of bustling priests and the animals destined for sacrifice. The disciples were like others of their day. They took pride in their Judaism. They also took great delight in the Temple of Jerusalem. Few structures in the world could rival it for its beauty and none for what it represented. The Temple was the pride of the first-century Jew. Perhaps overcome with national pride they pointed to the complex and remarked on its grandeur. Matthew 24 records the details of the conversation. Jesus' reaction was not what the disciples expected. "Do you not see all these things? Truly I say to you, not one stone here will be left upon another, which will not be torn down" (v. 2).

Torn down? One massive stone toppled from another? It didn't seem possible, but Jesus made the truth clear. He led the group down a path and across the Kidron Valley to the Mount of Olives. I imagine they made the walk in stunned silence as the disciples tried to make sense of the statement. Jesus let his words settle in. Once across the valley, Jesus sat down with His face turned to the Temple, which He could see in the distance.

Mustering their courage, the disciples asked the question that had been burning like a coal in their mind. "Tell us, when will these things happen, and what will be the sign of Your coming, and of the end of the age?" (Matthew 24:3). It was an important and loaded question—two questions really.

First, the disciples were looking for an immediate establish-
ment of the Kingdom. Perhaps they awoke each morning,
wondering if this was the day Jesus would bring to reality the
hope of every Jew. They wanted to know when He would
establish the Kingdom, and by that, they meant the earthly
Kingdom. They also wanted to know when Jesus' prophecy
regarding the Temple would happen. It made no sense to
them. What good was a Messianic Kingdom if there was no
Temple?

Jesus answered both their questions. He gave a long
answer, and at its heart is the reminder of the mystery of
lawlessness. He began by saying, "See to it that no one
misleads you" (v. 4). The mystery of lawlessness is always
about misleading. The serpent in the Garden misled Eve; in
Jesus' day others would come claiming to be Him or greater
than He. In the church age, false teachers plagued (and still
plague) congregations. In the future, the Antichrist will rise
and mislead many. Only awareness can ward off such delu-
sions.

After describing the world in upheaval, Jesus informs the
disciples that they will be delivered into tribulation. They will
be killed. Hatred will haunt the church and its members. And
that was just the beginning.

What Paul wrote the Thessalonians about the "lawless
one," Jesus spoke of on the hillside outside Jerusalem. "Many
false prophets will arise and will mislead many. Because
lawlessness is increased, most people's love will grow cold"
(vv. 11-12).

Lawlessness is not a single event. It didn't begin and end in
the Garden, nor is it confined to the future. In AD 70, the
Romans tore down the Temple, toppling its stone walls and
leaving heaps of rubble. They burned what they could, and in
the place where Jews had worshipped and made sacrifices to
God, the Romans erected standards, images of Caesar for all
to see—a Caesar Romans worshipped as a god. The Temple
had been desecrated.

That is the unpleasant point of the mystery of lawlessness:
It not only stands in opposition to the faith, it wishes to see it

destroyed and degraded. Such a travesty as that which occurred in AD 70 is hard for the modern mind to grasp. Even more difficult to comprehend is what is to come.

The Antichrist has been the subject of many discussions. Despite centuries of speculation on possible scenarios, we still know very little. Paul told the Thessalonians that the "lawless one" would work in accordance with Satan, the accuser. Under his direction and with his power, the Antichrist will work signs and false wonders. Many will fall away, just as Jesus said.

So how should we approach this subject? Bible scholars speak of "exegesis" and "eisegesis." Exegesis is the process of reading a document and taking from it the intended meaning. It means to "read out." Eisegesis is the opposite. It is the reader reading into the text, a dangerous practice. In no other area of biblical study does eisegesis appear so frequently as in eschatology (the study of end times). It is full of pitfalls. Many scholars have gone too far in their analysis of the text and the conclusions they draw—predicting the date and circum-stances of Christ's return—only to find their reputation damaged.

The biblical revelation about the man of lawlessness, the Antichrist, is worthy of serious study, but conjecture should be avoided. The list of people once thought to be the Antichrist is long and includes Nero, Hitler, Mussolini, Stalin, American presidents, White House staff, and Roman popes. To date all such guesses have been wrong. Such guesswork, no matter how erroneous, cannot negate the fact that some-one called the "lawless one" will come, and he will be the culmination of lawlessness that began in the Garden of Eden and that will continue until Christ comes again.

CONFLICT

When the apostle John uses the term *antichrist,* he was not always referring to a specific individual. "Children, it is the last hour; and just as you heard that antichrist is coming, even now many antichrists have appeared; from this we know that it is the last hour" (1 John 2:18). (Note that both present and future tense are used.) Some have assumed that the term *antichrist* means "the opposite of Jesus the Christ." An antichrist is not the opposite of Jesus but someone who works in opposition to Him. There have been many antichrists. John's primary reference isn't to the one person in the future who will rise to power, but to anyone who does "not acknowledge Jesus Christ as coming in the flesh. This is the deceiver and the antichrist" (2 John 1:7). One of the Gnostic doctrines was that deity could not dwell in human flesh; therefore, Jesus could not be the God-man He claimed to be.

The true Antichrist will follow the same pattern of denial. While not new, such heresies will crescendo to a level never before seen. The Antichrist will reach the pinnacle of his power after Christ gathers the church to meet Him in the air, during which time the Holy Spirit and His restraining ministry will be withdrawn. Lawlessness will then expand unchecked, ending only with the second coming of Christ.

This world leader, influenced and enabled by Satan, will do battle against all that is holy. It is a battle that he is destined to lose, but one he will wage nonetheless. The good news is that Jesus "will slay [him] with the breath of His mouth and bring to an end by the appearance of His coming" (2 Thessalonians 2:8).

The future Antichrist has another name: "son of perdition/destruction." The word *perdition* conveys the sense of laying waste, putting to ruin, or destining to destruction. The word appears twenty times in the New Testament, but the phrase "son of destruction" only twice.

The phrase is first used in one of Jesus' prayers. He says, "While I was with them, I was keeping them in Your name which You have given Me; and I guarded them and not one of them perished but the son of perdition, so that the Scripture would be fulfilled" (John 17:12). The reference is to Judas Iscariot, the world's most infamous traitor. Judas was destined to destruction and so is the Antichrist. The battle will be great, the effort powerful, but in the end, Jesus will win and we will win with Him.

IN THE FACE OF EVIL

Jesus foretold of evil but also promised victory. The mystery
of lawlessness is that sin has been with us since the beginning and will remain until Christ comes again to establish
His earthly Kingdom. It is the norm for our world. That
leaves us in the middle of a corrupt environment. Sin may
have entered the world in the Garden but it did not end there;
it continued to grow, infecting the world.

Every year, millions of people come down with some strain
of the influenza virus. Most experience only a few days of
discomfort. Others are more dramatically affected. Historians
note that large-scale outbreaks occurred in centuries past.
The years 1510, 1557, and 1580 all saw severe and deadly
outbreaks. Pandemics occurred in 1729, 1732, and three times
in the 1800s. The worst and most deadly bout, however, took
place in 1918–1919. Sometimes called the Spanish flu, the
virus killed twenty million people, more than double the
number lost in World War I, which had just ended. (Oddly,
those most affected were young adults under forty, the age
group usually thought least likely to feel the impact of a widespread virus.)

Lawlessness–sin–is similar to a pandemic. While always
present, there are times when it reaches unexpected heights
of destruction. Sin is not a virus, but it does spread throughout humanity and can be a deadly spiritual infection.

Lawlessness has always been; lawlessness is evident now,
and lawlessness will continue until Christ comes again–the
worst is yet to come. The only solution to the pandemic of sin
is faith in Christ. There have been many antichrists and there
will be more. There will be one–the lawless one, the son of
perdition–who will lead the world into a tribulation that is
almost impossible to imagine.

Should we worry about the future? Should we study the
news to see what political leader best meets the description of
the Antichrist? Should we formulate expansive scenarios in
anticipation of the coming Tribulation? No. Our call is to be
alert and to remain grounded in our faith. God has not
chosen to reveal everything that is to happen. He has given us

enough to be forewarned and alert. The best we can do is avoid lawlessness by exemplifying lawfulness; that is, to show the change Christ makes in our life.

As Peter instructed the beleaguered believers of the first century:

> *Who is there to harm you if you prove zealous for what is good? But even if you should suffer for the sake of righteousness, you are blessed. And do not fear their intimidation, and do not be troubled, but sanctify Christ as Lord in your hearts, always being ready to make a defense to everyone who asks you to give an account for the hope that is in you, yet with gentleness and reverence; and keep a good conscience so that in the thing in which you are slandered, those who revile your good behavior in Christ will be put to shame. For it is better, if God should will it so, that you suffer for doing what is right rather than for doing what is wrong. (1 Peter 3:13-17)*

False prophets will arise. They always have; they always will. It is incumbent upon us to know what we believe and why we believe it, confident in the knowledge that one day lawlessness will be vanquished. "Despite the fact that evil has not given up the struggle, and will not do so until the very end, the kingdom of God works and progresses, not *towards* victory, but *from* the platform of victory already achieved."[4]

Yes, the worst is yet to come, yet God in His mercy has revealed that the best is yet to come as well—and ultimately, for those in Christ's Kingdom, the best will never end.

FOR REFLECTION

1. Describe the conditions in the church of Thessalonica that led Paul to discuss lawlessness with them in 2 Thessalonians 2:7-10.
2. In what ways does the Holy Spirit restrain lawlessness today?
3. What do we learn from Ephesians 6:11-12 about defending ourselves against evil with the Holy Spirit's help?
4. In 1 John 2:18-22, the apostle John discusses the "many

antichrists" who have tried to deceive the church. Compare their activity with that of the Antichrist who will rise to power in the end times.

5. Discuss the mystery of lawlessness. What does it tell us about "normal conditions" that believers must expect to face in this world?

A FINAL WORD

The Ready Revealer of Secrets

P HILIP Yancey starts his book *The Jesus I Never Knew* with a quote from G. K. Chesterton:

Suppose we hear an unknown man spoken of by many men. Suppose we were puzzled to hear that some men said he was too tall and some too short; some objected to his fatness, some lamented his leanness; some thought him too dark, and some too fair. One explanation . . . would be that he might be an odd shape. But there is another explanation. He might be the right shape. . . . Perhaps (in short) this extraordinary thing is really the ordinary thing; at least the normal thing, the centre.[1]

Biblical interpretation is never easy. In Jesus' day, congregations had to puzzle over parables and stew over sermons. Some may have become impatient with the process, deeming the truth unworthy of the effort. To them the teaching was too long, or too short, or too critical, or not critical enough. Perhaps the parables seemed too hard and the mysteries too deep. Like the man described by Chesterton, the teachings of Christ may appear in an unexpected form, different from what we might expect. At times, we may wish that God had just used e-mail. Things would be much simpler then. Or would they?

The mysteries of God, the secrets He held until just the right time, are gifts. Like many gifts, they have to be unwrapped and examined. Wouldn't it be easier if God said, "Look, here's what I mean," and then sent another book our way? It might be easier, but it wouldn't be nearly as meaningful. Bible study is work. We do not read the Bible like a novel or the front page of a newspaper. Its words are loaded, its phrases filled with layers of meaning.

In this book, we have taken a single word–*mystery*–and tracked it through the New Testament. Some truths were easy to see; others required that we camp in their vicinity and, like an archeologist, dust off one layer of revelation after another. Is God being obtuse? Is He attempting to hide His truth from His children? No. He has made it all clear enough, but effort is needed and in that effort is the reward.

God has kept His secrets and then revealed them to the world. Those secrets, those mysteries, are not in the Bible to befuddle us, but to engage us, and having engaged us, to empower us. There is value in the process of discovery as well as in the learning of truth. Paul bubbled over with joy at the thought: "Oh, the depth of the riches both of the wisdom and knowledge of God! How unsearchable are His judgments and unfathomable His ways!" (Romans 11:33).

His ways are inscrutable. We would know very little about our God if He chose to hide Himself. But our God is the Ready Revealer of secrets. He has made Himself known–not all at once, but bit by necessary bit. Those bits are precious and for our benefit.

The world is fascinated with discovering life on other planets, as if in finding some microbe on Jupiter's moon Io or a protein strand in the sands of Mars, we will somehow vindicate our own existence. We have spent millions of dollars listening through electronic ears to the sounds of distant space and peering at distant stars, searching for planets that circle their own sun. We wonder: Is intelligent life out there? What would it say to us? Extraterrestrial life does exist and He has made contact. A Being greater than any life–indeed the Creator of that life–has reached out and touched us. That message is in the inspired words of the Bible, laid out for any interested person to read and to study. In study is adventure.

We stand on the platform of privilege, able to look back to Creation and follow God's work through the centuries. We peer back with an understanding that many in Old Testament days would envy.

The question is, what will we do with these truths?

The longest and most intricate psalm in the Bible is Psalm 119. It's an elaborate bundle of 176 verses divided into twenty-two stanzas of eight lines. A different Hebrew letter begins each stanza. If composed in English, the first eight verses would all begin with the letter *A*, the next eight with the letter *B*, etc. Such a long alphabetic acrostic is difficult to create, but the psalmist did just that. And what was his topic? The Word of God. He wrote:

> *O how I love Your law!*
> *It is my meditation all the day.*
> *Your commandments make me wiser than my enemies,*
> *For they are ever mine.*
> *I have more insight than all my teachers,*
> *For Your testimonies are my meditation.*
> *I understand more than the aged,*
> *Because I have observed Your precepts.*
> *I have restrained my feet from every evil way,*
> *That I may keep Your word.*
> *I have not turned aside from Your ordinances,*
> *For You Yourself have taught me.*
> *How sweet are Your words to my taste!*
> *Yes, sweeter than honey to my mouth!*
> *From Your precepts I get understanding;*
> *Therefore I hate every false way. (vv. 97-104)*

The mysteries of God are not meant to be an academic pursuit, they are meant to change lives—our lives. The more we know the more different we become.

God has shown His love in countless ways. One way is this: He has let us in on His secrets. And unlike other secrets, He meant for us to share in them.

FOR REFLECTION

1. Many Christians wish God had more clearly spelled out the truths about His Kingdom and His plan for the world in the Bible. After reading this book, do you have a greater appreciation for God's "mysteries" as a way to gain greater intimacy with God? Why or why not?

2. Which "mystery" discussed in this book has been most significant for you personally? How has your understanding of God, other people, or yourself changed as a result of what you've learned?

Introduction: Where's the Mystery?

1 See http://www.hubblesite.org.

2 Mark uses the singular *mystery.*

3 See http://www.temple.edu/about/temples_founder.html.

Chapter 1: Why Does God Keep Secrets?

1 Richard Felix, *The School of Dying Graces* (Wheaton, Ill.: Tyndale House, 2004), 106–107; italics appear in original text.

2 J. I. Packer, *Knowing God* (Downers Grove, Ill.: InterVarsity Press, 1973), 21.

3 John Eldredge, *Waking the Dead: The Glory of a Heart Fully Alive* (Nashville: Thomas Nelson, 2003), 23–24.

Chapter 2: The Mystery of God's Will

1 Alice Calaprice, ed., *The Quotable Einstein* (Princeton, N.J.: Princeton University Press, 1966), 161.

2 Ronald W. Clark, *Einstein: The Life and Times* (New York: The World Publishing Co., 1971), 19.

3 G. Campbell Morgan, "Introduction," in *God's Perfect Will* (Willow Grove, Penn.: Woodlawn Electronic Publishing, 1998).

4 Ralph P. Martin, "Ephesians," in *The Broadman Bible Commentary,* ed. Clifton Allen, 135 (Nashville: Broadman Press, 1971).

5 Flavius Josephus and William Whiston, *The Works of Josephus: Complete and Unabridged* (Peabody, Mass.: Hendrickson, 1980).

6 C. S. Lewis, *Mere Christianity* (San Francisco: HarperSanFrancisco, 2001), 133.

7 C. S. Lewis, *The Lion, the Witch and the Wardrobe* (New York: The MacMillan Company, 1950), 149.

8 Ibid., 160.

9 The New Living Translation expresses Ephesians 1:10 this way: "This is the plan: At the right time he will bring everything together under the authority of Christ."

10 Timothy George, "The Big Picture," *This We Believe* (Grand Rapids: Zondervan, 2000), 222.

11 C. S. Lewis, *The Great Divorce* (New York: MacMillan, 1946), 72.

12 Examples include 1 Corinthians 1:1, 2 Corinthians 1:1, and Ephesians 1:1.

13 Gracia Burnham with Dean Merrill, *In the Presence of My Enemies* (Wheaton, Ill.: Tyndale House Publishers, 2003), 261–263.

14 A. W. Tozer, *The Pursuit of God* (Camp Hill, Penn.: Christian Publications, Inc.), 92.

Chapter 3: Jesus: The Mega Mystery

1 Acts 11:26 says, "And for an entire year [Barnabas and Paul] met with the church and taught considerable numbers; and the disciples were first called Christians in Antioch."

[2] Philip Yancey, *The Jesus I Never Knew* (Grand Rapids: Zondervan, 1995), 36–37.

[3] See Acts 21:26ff and Ephesians 2:14-18.

[4] Eric Reed, "Leadership Weekly," the electronic newsletter of *Leadership Journal,* April 13, 2004.

Chapter 4: The Kingdom of God and of Heaven

[1] Geoffrey W. Bromiley, ed. *The International Standard Bible Encyclopedia,* vol. K–P (Grand Rapids: Eerdmans, 1986), 27.

[2] John Piper, "Compassion, Power, and the Kingdom of God," from a sermon delivered February 4, 1990, and accessed at http://www.desiringgod.org/library/sermons/90/020490.html.

[3] John does record Jesus' dialogue with Pilate in which He reveals that His kingdom is not of this world. See John 18:28-40.

[4] As quoted in *The New Encyclopedia of Christian Quotations,* compiled by Mark Water (Grand Rapids: Baker, 2000).

[5] Malcolm Muggeridge, *Jesus Rediscovered* (New York: Doubleday, 1979), 47–48; quoted in Max Lucado, *When God Whispers Your Name* (Nashville: W Publishing Group, 1999).

[6] As quoted in David Mills, "Years the Locust Have Eaten: Malcolm Muggeridge's *Chronicles of Wasted Time* as an Apology of Wasted Love," *Touchstone* (December 2003), 35.

[7] Malcolm Muggeridge, *Confessions of a Twentieth-Century Pilgrim* (San Francisco: Harper & Row, 1988). Accessed at http://ic.net/erasmust/RAZ83.HTM.

[8] Frederick Buechner, *Listening to Your Life: Daily Meditations with Frederick Buechner,* compiled by George Connor (San Francisco: HarperSanFrancisco, 1992), 303–304.

Chapter 5: The Perplexity of Parables

[1] Luci Shaw, "Bridging the Gap: How Story Shapes Our Thoughts about God" (lecture, Calvin College Festival of Faith and Writing, April 22, 2004).

[2] Ibid.

[3] See Matthew 12:1-2; 12:22-24; 9:18, 24; and 12:38-39.

[4] Richard Bewes, *The Stone That Became a Mountain: Getting It Right about the Kingdom of God* (Ross-shire, Great Britain: Christian Focus Publications, 2001), 60–61.

Chapter 6: Seeds, Dirt, Weeds, and Birds

[1] Jesus does tell other short parables earlier in Matthew but these were not specifically related to the Kingdom of Heaven teaching. In fact, some argue that they are not true parables but metaphors and similes.

[2] Lee Dye, "Life from Old Seeds" at http://www.abcnews.go.com/sections/scitech/DyeHard/dyehard020314.html.

[3] Jack Cavanaugh, *The Puritans* (Colorado Springs: Victor Books, 1994), 171–172.

[4] In the terminology of first-century Palestinian farmers, this phrase means that between thirty and one hundred times as many seeds would be harvested as had been sown. The average yield then was tenfold. See Craig S. Keener, *The IVP Bible Background Commentary: New Testament* (Downers Grove, Ill.: InterVarsity Press, 1993), 82.

Chapter 7: That Tares It

[1] Information about Frank Abagnale can be found at his Web site http://www.abagnale.com.

[2] C. S. Lewis, *The Case for Christianity* (New York: Collier Books, 1943), 56.

ENDNOTES

Chapter 8: A Little Mustard Is a Good Thing

[1] http://www.guinnessworldrecords.com/

[2] Microsoft® Encarta® Reference Library 2003. © 1993–2002 Microsoft Corporation. All rights reserved.

[3] C. S. Lewis, *The Screwtape Letters* (New York: Collier Books, 1982), 12.

[4] See OMF Web site http://www.omf.org/content.asp?id=9972.

Chapter 9: The Yeast We Can Do

[1] See Leviticus 7:13 and Amos 4:5.

[2] Acts 1:8. See also Matthew 28:19.

[3] Calvin Miller, *The Table of Inwardness* (Downers Grove, Ill.: InterVarsity Press, 1984), 22.

[4] Malcolm Muggeridge, *Jesus: The Man Who Lives* (New York: Harper & Row, 1975), 144.

[5] Herschel Hobbs, *The Illustrated Life of Jesus* (Nashville, Tenn.: Holman Bible Publishers, 2000), 108.

Chapter 10: Treasure Hunter

[1] See Psalm 53:1 and Romans 3:12.

Chapter 11: Net Profits

[1] These are the kinds of nets Peter and Simon left behind when Jesus called them to be disciples. Mark 1:16-18.

[2] *Dragnet* is the term used in Matthew 13:47 in the New American Standard Bible and the New King James version. Other translations simply say "net" or "fishing net."

[3] Louis Berkof, "The Attributes of God," *The Living God, Readings in Christian Theology,* ed. Millard J. Erickson (Grand Rapids: Baker Books, 1973), 358.

[4] Ibid.

[5] Chuck Colson, *Answers to Your Kids' Questions* (Wheaton, Ill.: Tyndale House, 2000), 31–32.

[6] From a sermon John Piper gave on February 4, 1990, entitled "Compassion, Power, and the Kingdom of God" See http://www.desiringgod.org/library/ sermons/ 90/ 020490.html.

Chapter 12: The Mystery of the Gospel

[1] See http://www.scripturecandy.com/ourstory.htm.

[2] *The Theological Dictionary of the New Testament*, "euangelion." Gerhard Kittel and others, eds. (Grand Rapids: Eerdmans, 1964), s.v.

[3] Richard Bewes, *The Stone That Became a Mountain: Getting It Right about the Kingdom of God* (Ross-shire, Great Britain: Christian Focus Publication, 2001), 36.

[4] John 18:33-38

Chapter 13: The Mystery of the Church

[1] Kenneth S. Wuest, *The New Testament: An Expanded Translation.* From the electronic edition; first published in three volumes as *Expanded Translation of the Greek New Testament*, Matt. 16:13 (Grand Rapids, Mich.: Eerdmans, 1961).

[2] Warren W. Wiersbe, *The Bible Exposition Commentary* (Wheaton, Ill.: Victor Books, 1989).

[3] Andrew Murray, *Prayer: A 31-Day Plan to Enrich Your Prayer Life* (Uhrichsville, Ohio: Barbour, 1995).

[4] This verse is often confused with 1 Corinthians 6:19: "Do you not know that your body is a temple of the Holy Spirit who is in you . . . ?" This verse is in the singular and refers to the believer's body, while 1 Corinthians 3:16 is in the plural and that, along with the context, tells us that Paul is speaking of the church.

[5] See Matthew 21:42; Mark 12:10; Luke 20:17; Acts 4:11; and 1 Peter 2:7.

[6] Paul Lee Tan, *Encyclopedia of 7700 Illustrations* (Dallas: Bible Communications, 1979).

[7] See Revelation 6:17 and Revelation 11.

[8] Martyn Lloyd-Jones, *Revival* (Wheaton, Ill.: Good News Publishers/Crossway Books, 1987).

Chapter 14: The Mystery of Israel

[1] Craig S. Keener, *The IVP Bible Background Commentary: New Testament*, Rom. 11:15 (Downers Grove, Ill.: InterVarsity Press, 1993).

[2] John F. Walvoord and Roy B. Zuck, eds., *The Bible Knowledge Commentary: An Exposition of the Scriptures* (Wheaton, Ill.: Victor Books, 1983), 482.

[3] See Exodus 7:3 to read what God told Moses. Exodus 8:15, 32; and 9:34 describe the three occasions on which Pharaoh hardened his heart.

[4] Walvoord and Zuck, *The Bible Knowledge Commentary: An Exposition of the Scriptures*, 482.

Chapter 15: The Mystery of Lawlessness

[1] F. F. Bruce, *Word Biblical Commentary: 1 and 2 Thessalonians*, vol. 45 (Waco, Tex.: Word Books, 1982), 161.

[2] Herschel Hobbs, *The Broadman Bible Commentary*, vol. 11, ed. Clifton Allen (Nashville: Broadman Press, 1971), 291.

[3] For a more detailed discussion of the identity of the serpent see Alton Gansky's *Uncovering the Bible's Greatest Mysteries* (Nashville: Broadman & Holman, 2002).

[4] Richard Bewes, *The Stone That Became a Mountain: Getting It Right about the Kingdom of God* (Ross-shire, Great Britain: Christian Focus Publication, 2001), 104.

A Final Word: The Ready Revealer of Secrets

[1] Philip Yancey, *The Jesus I Never Knew* (Grand Rapids, Mich.: Zondervan, 1995), 12.

<u>FREE Discussion Guide for *The Secrets God Kept*!</u>

A discussion guide written by

John Van Diest

is available at

 ChristianBookGuides.com